GOD'S INVITATION FOR YOU AWAITS

GOD'S INVITATION FOR YOU AWAITS

Naylee Bartlett

Pinsan Books

Copyright © 2018 Naylee Bartlett

All rights reserved.

ISBN: 978-0-9956823-1-3

CONTENTS

	Introduction	1
1	God Knows You	5
2	God Has A Purpose For You	16
3	God Has Gifted You	24
4	God Created The World Around You	37
5	God Made The Earth Just Perfect For You	47
6	He Supplies All Your Needs	53
7	Jesus Said, "You Must Be Born Again"	57
8	The Lord Jesus Is The Only One Who Can Complete You	75
9	The Lord Jesus Is Preparing A Mansion For You In Heaven	82
10	Are You Coming To God's Party? You Are Invited	90
11	It's Very, Very Rude To Decline The Lord's Invitation	110
12	Be Ready For The Day Of The Lord	118
13	Why Do People Blame God?	126
14	Make Every Effort To Be Heaven's Resident	143
15	Your Benefits Here On Earth As You Believe In God's Word	152

INTRODUCTION

"Come to Me, all you who labour and weary and are heavy laden, and I will give you rest. Take My yoke upon you and learn from Me, for I am gentle and lowly in heart, and you will find rest for your souls. For My yoke is easy and My burden is light" (Matthew 11:28–30). This is the first invitation I could suggest the Lord Jesus wants all people to respond to, to come to Him, which means to know Him.

Do you feel stressed out in life? Do you feel you're carrying all the responsibility at work, and at home, especially if you're a single mum or single dad? Most of us work, whether it's a heavy or light job, and it can easily stress us out, with the daily grind of life; but the Lord Jesus knows all these burdens in life we face every day. That's why the Lord Jesus is offering you to: "Come to Him and learn from Him." Being in His presence eases the tiredness of your soul; you can rely on Him. You can rest assured He cares for you, because He loves you. He could take away the pain, in your soul. His peace is not an ordinary peace; it's a peace that's so deep it's soothing to one's soul. When He said, "My yoke is easy, My burden is light," He's informing you when you're yoked with Him, it lightens the load you're carrying so it's not too heavy for you. And you can rely on Jesus who is yoked with you, because He feels what you feel. (The Lord said, "For I am gentle and lowly in heart.")

When you feel the peace of God, it's so encompassing to your senses; it makes you feel that you want that feeling all the time. It's unexplainable in human terms.

God understands your needs. If you're a parent you may make the comparison with the level of care and love you gave your children, and that gentle approach and soft heart towards them. In a similar way the Lord Jesus is offering you help because He treats us as His children.

So that's what the Lord Jesus is offering you today; to unload your physical, mental, and emotional stresses on Him, because He loves you and cares for you.

As the days and years go by, I realise that there is one thing I couldn't live without; and that is to be loved. No one could live a

INTRODUCTION

life without love! When we know we are loved by our parents, family members, and people around us, and that we are valued by our parents and affirmed that we belong to them, no matter what, whether we make a mistake or our loved ones are not proud of our choices in life, then we have the assurance that we are still accepted by them and always will be connected to them, being blood relatives. And the saying that blood is thicker than water is true. We wouldn't be neglected or pushed aside just because we made a few mistakes in life. We have their support and value because they are our family members; we draw strength from them because we are related to them. We know we can trust them with all our hearts, and expect them to care for us and maybe give us a word of encouragement to support us, whatever we are facing in life.

But some people might say, "I didn't have that kind of care and upbringing in life. I was hated. I was not loved. No one cares about me. I was abandoned when I was little. I was orphaned. I was put in a home when I was very young. I was neglected. I was adopted. I was abused by my own parents and I was ashamed; I hated them and they hated me." And maybe you're asking yourself, "Why was I even born? No one shows me any care and affection. I'm depressed and I'm so longing to be loved; I just want someone to love me. What's the point of life?" You might not believe me now, but I can tell you that God truly and deeply cares for you, and loves you.

Even though you might have had these awful experiences, at least once or twice in your life someone must have been good to you. I am sure that someone along the way in life must have picked you up and cared for you, or even cradled you, and you remembered this later in life. But if you could never remember anyone loving you, God Himself loves you.

The world (everything) rotates because of love, and true love, originates from God Himself, and He created us through His great love for us! Whether you know it or not, the Lord Jesus loves you and wants you to be with Him in heaven. Love is the action that binds people together. You are very important to God and He loved you so much that He gave life to you.

Whatever experiences you may have, we all have one thing in common: we will all die one day, and death is the final

INTRODUCTION

destination on earth of every living being. You might say, "That is *so* depressing." But I want you to take heart, for the Lord Jesus is preparing a place for you in heaven. In the Bible He said, "*In My Father's house are many mansions, and I come to prepare a place for you there, so that you can be with Me.*"

The Lord Jesus' invitation does not have an expiry date, but there is urgency while you are still alive, because it involves the future of every single person living on earth, and because we know that every living soul or person will die one day—no one will live forever on earth. So it is only a matter of time before we say goodbye to this planet earth, and **death is the final destination of all**.

The first time the Lord Jesus came to earth was to show His love and save the world, but when He returns He will judge the whole world. Because one day all that is on the earth will be burned up with fervent heat, and He wants you to escape from the judgement that is coming on earth when He comes for the second time—as He has said in His word. That's why the Lord Jesus has an invitation for you. His invitation is to have a relationship with Him and to know Him, and to know God the Father, and God the Holy Spirit.

The final destination of everyone on earth is death, that's why the Lord Jesus has invited us to have eternal life with Him.

1

GOD KNOWS YOU

*"Before **I** formed you in the womb **I** knew you; before you were born **I** sanctified you; I ordained you a prophet to the nations."* (This was God talking to Jeremiah—see Jeremiah 1:5.) God knows you and He created you. How can I say this? Well, let me explain why. The reason I know why the Lord knows you is because He knows me, and He speaks to me and I am alive today in 2018. If God knows me He knows you too. You may ask, "How do you know that God knows you?" Well, He answers my prayers and I could hear Him and He hears me. He will answer your prayers too.

And I am an ordinary person just like you. You may be holding a higher position in the community, as we say in the Philippines 'a big shot', but we are all created by God, and created equal, immaterial of our job position, community position, title, or even the colour of our skin.

Let me give you three examples of why I know the Lord knows you, and cares so much about you:

1. In the Bible, in 1 Samuel 4:12–22, when Samuel the prophet was little, the Lord called his name, "Samuel, Samuel," a few times. Samuel didn't know the Lord God by then, because he was only a child, but his mother, Hannah, was a believer in God. Hannah had dedicated him to God before he was even created in her womb (some people may think that is so in excess of devotion because it's like the child doesn't have any say or freedom) but she was barren and so she made a vow to God when she asked for a son.

Her husband Elkannah had two wives: Peninah and Hannah. Year after year, they had to go to Jerusalem to join the rest of the Israelites for a yearly sacrifice. And because Hannah was barren, Peninah, her rival, had so taunted her year after year in front of Elkannah and her children. So you can imagine the bitterness in her soul when she was being laughed at and taunted by the other woman and her children, in front of other people that were with them.

Though she was much loved by Elkannah, and he showed much affection to her in front of other people around them, that didn't stop her from feeling not included, or incomplete; especially as women in her generation were considered accursed if they couldn't bear children. (I am sure every ordinary woman would be weeping too.)

This made Hannah so depressed that she asked God for a son and promised God that she would give her son in service for the Lord—to do God's work in the Lord's temple as long as he lived. The Lord saw Hannah's heart, and granted her requests, so that's what she did.

In God's temple, when Samuel was a bit older, God called out to him (1 Samuel 3: 4–12): *Then the Lord called Samuel, and he said, "Here I am!" and ran to Eli and said, "Here I am, for you called me." But he said, "I did not call; lie down again." So he went and lay down.*

And the Lord called again, "Samuel!" and Samuel arose and went to Eli and said, "Here I am, for you called me." But he said, "I did not call, my son; lie down again." Now Samuel did not yet know the Lord, and the word of the Lord had not yet been revealed to him.

And the Lord called Samuel again the third time. And he arose and went to Eli and said, "Here I am, for you called me." Then Eli perceived that the Lord was calling the young man. Therefore Eli said to Samuel, "Go, lie down, and if He calls you, you shall say, 'Speak, Lord, for your servant hears.'" So Samuel went and lay down in his place.

And the Lord came and stood, calling as at other times, "Samuel! Samuel!" And Samuel said, "Speak, for your servant hears." Then the Lord said to Samuel, "Behold, I am about to do a thing in Israel at which the two ears of everyone who hears it will tingle. On that day I will fulfil against Eli all that I have spoken concerning his house, from beginning to end.

So the Lord couldn't have called Samuel if He didn't know him. You may think: they were the prophets and Kings so the

Lord knows them, but the Lord God established all of us on earth.

2. Some years ago, I heard a story on a radio programme about a little girl who became an orphan at the age of five. Her parents were both drug addicts and alcoholics. One night at their home, her dad got so angry with her mum that he stabbed her in front of this child. Then he came to his senses, when the mother of his child he had just stabbed stopped moving and fighting and actually died due to the deep wounds he had inflicted on her. He sobbed, and knowing she was dead, he killed himself in front of his little girl who was very scared and bewildered. Not knowing what to do she sobbed and sobbed.

Eventually a social worker found out what had happened to this family, and the child was put up for adoption. Fortunately for this little girl, the couple who adopted her were both born-again Christians, and they brought her to church one Sunday morning. The adoptive mum whispered to the Sunday school teacher to go easy on her, because she had never been to a Sunday school meeting, or a church, before.

The Sunday school teacher's lesson on that particular day was about the miracle of the Lord Jesus' feeding the five thousand men (not counting the women and children), from the five loaves of bread and two fishes available. When all the people had eaten and were satisfied, there were twelve basketfuls of left-overs.

The Sunday school teacher then asked the children, holding up a picture, "Who can tell me who this man is?" To the Sunday school teacher's surprise, this little orphan girl put her hand up and said, "I do ... I do..." sobbing. "He was the man who was holding my hand when my dad killed my mum, before he killed himself in front of me."

This little girl had never seen the Lord Jesus in any picture before but she recognised Him as the man who held her hand at that fateful event, when she saw both her parents die, due to the awful effects of drugs and alcohol.

I could just imagine the tears the Lord Jesus shed over this child when she lost both of her parents on that awful evening. She must have been so scared—all alone and without hope. But with the Lord Jesus holding her, He must have quietened and cradled her in His loving arms. When she didn't even know what was going on in her life, the Lord Jesus held her and rescued her and comforted her. Only He, the Lord Jesus, knew how to ease the emotional pain and hopelessness and despair of this little girl.

When I heard this on the radio I could not stop crying for this little girl's experience. I totally believe the story, even though the testimony was told by the presenter, and not by the girl. I think it was way back in the mid 90's or early 2000's.

So you see, this little girl recognised the Lord Jesus, and so the Lord Jesus must have known this girl, as He held her hand.

You see how loving and faithful and good God is? In Psalm 34:18 it says: *The Lord is close to the broken hearted and saves those who are crushed in spirit.* It truly shows in this story of the little girl—how He comforted her in the time she needed God. This has really taught me that God cares deeply for all who are in distress and have no hope.

3. And this is my own experience, when I was a teenager working in a café in 1976:

Whenever the son of the boss would be coming home from Manila, to visit his parents, where my sister, who works as a beautician in their parlour, and I were working and living in the same house as them, I would hear this voice telling me, "Robert is coming." Every time I heard this voice he would arrive without fail on that day. Normally he would phone his mother letting her know he was coming, but sometimes he would just turn up without telling anyone he was coming home from Manila. After I heard this voice for a few times, I was wondering if other people heard a voice like I did. And one time when I heard this voice again I told my sister, "Robert is coming today." My sister said, "Let's see," and told the other beauticians with her. Our lady employer overheard her and said, "Yes he is." "Oh, by the way, how did you know?" She replied, "I don't know, Naylee told me." "And how did she know?" "I don't know she replied, ask her." But no one asked me so I didn't have to explain to them about the voice I was hearing. He did turn up on that evening and my sister told me that it was my mental telepathy that I knew he was coming on that day. But I wasn't actually thinking about him visiting his parents, I just heard a voice, which sounded peaceful and comforting, almost like teasing me to make me feel joyful, because I had a crush on him. I heard this voice, that's what I know, and was really wondering if I was the only one hearing this voice.

Life goes on for me and I became a born-again Christian believer in 1982. Life brings challenges and at one point in my life, when I was here in England, I sinned against the Lord, big time, in my eyes, but not in God's eyes; as I realised when I was remorseful and telling the Lord why I did it, which was just to get my own back on someone.

You hear people say, revenge is sweet; but in my case I am the one that felt defeated, because I knew the goodness of God in my life yet I took revenge on an unbeliever. I said to myself, "O Lord, how could I claim that I am a Christian when I did exactly as unbelievers would do? I was so remorseful.

After sinning I asked the Lord, "Lord can You forgive me? Do You still love me, now that I've sinned against You? I haven't got anyone but You; if You turn Your back on me, how could I live? Though I've sinned, You are still my everything." But I felt the Lord was listening to me; He was right there in the same room as I was. Then I heard a whisper... "Do you really think that was your mental telepathy?" Reminding me of the past, I recognised the voice, exactly the same as the one I used to hear when Robert was coming home from Manila to see his parents. "Oh Lord, it's You all along." I clasped my hand over my mouth; I was shocked that God had been there for me all the time. I couldn't imagine—I had a secret, yet loving, observer watching every step, mistake or success I had ever done. "O God," I said with a sigh.

Then the Lord revealed to me everything I ever experienced when I was little: My dog that went missing for a week and came back after I prayed. Even the second life the Lord granted that dog because God saw my tears.... The Lord even reminded me of the ring that I lost in the sea; again after I prayed, I found it. Both of these events were flashed back to me, and the feelings were brought back again as though I was in the same situation, just like when I was little. Also the time when my dad wanted to kill me, the voice I heard was the Lord's; He warned me not to pass on the small footpath or I would die. After all these revelations from God, I felt He was answering my questions by saying, "IF I LOVED YOU WHEN YOU WERE LITTLE, WHY WOULD I CHANGE NOW?" It was a complete assurance and acceptance of His love and forgiveness beyond my understanding. It was immense; I felt complete and accepted again.

So I know if God knows me He definitely knows you too. I am no different from anyone; I am as ordinary as any human being breathing air in their lungs. God knows when you were born, because He gave breath and life to you.

And it says in Psalm 139, headed with **God's Perfect Knowledge of Man**, verses 13–17: *For You formed my inward parts; You covered me in my mother's womb. I will praise You, for I am fearfully and wonderfully made; marvellous are Your works, and that my soul knows very well. My frame was not hidden from You, when I was made in secret, and skilfully wrought in the lowest parts of the earth. Your eyes saw my substance, being yet unformed. And in Your book* (the book of life) *they all were written, the days fashioned for me, when as yet there were none of them. How precious also are Your thoughts to me, O God! How great is the sum of them!*

If we go back to Psalm 139:1–4 it says: *You have searched me, Lord, and you know me. You know when I sit and when I rise; You perceive my thoughts from afar. You discern my going out and my lying down; You are familiar with all my ways. Before a word is on my tongue You, Lord, know it completely.*

So you see, according to these passages God created you. You might say, but they were written concerning those kings and prophets of long ago. If you really, really, want to know if God is for real then talk to Him, ask Him. What question would you want to ask Him? It's not just that He knows you, but He wants you to call on Him, for He says, *'Call to Me, and I will answer you, and show you great and mighty things, which you do not know'* (Jeremiah 33:3). He challenges people to call on Him.

Did you know that your name is written in heaven? The Lord Jesus said so, see Luke 10:20. This is what it says (His disciples talking to Him about healing of people and the Lord Jesus speaking to them, saying): *"However, do not rejoice that the* *spirits submit to you, but **rejoice that your names are written in heaven.***"

Also, in Exodus 32:31–33: *So Moses returned to the Lord and said, "Alas, this people has sinned a great sin. They have made for themselves gods of gold. But now, if you will forgive their sin—but if not, please blot me out of your book that you have written." But the Lord said to Moses, "Whoever has sinned against me, **I will blot out of My book**.* (So there is a book of life, or book of remembrance, in heaven.) You can never ever erase what was written, and what was not written you cannot jot in.

Have you heard of the song that goes, *Would you know my name if you saw me in heaven?* In this song the father of a little boy who died in an accident is asking a question, maybe in his heart, if his boy will know him as his dad in heaven. Some famous people know that there is heaven, especially for those with little children that died before them. And when you love someone, you want to know they will be in heaven with you when they die. But what about you, have you placed your life in His hands? **Only Jesus has the key to eternal life.**

God knows everything, and I can assure you, God knows you personally, see Psalm 121 (God the help of those who seek Him). You may say, "But I did not seek Him." Even though you did not seek Him, if you've got breath in your nostrils He knows you. Why? Because God assigned an Angel to guard you, especially the little children, because you're alive through the spirit He breathed on you when He placed you in your mother's womb. For it says in Matthew 18:10: *"Take heed that you do not despise one of these little ones, for I say to you that in heaven their angels always see the face of My Father who is in heaven.*

And in Psalm 91:11: *He will charge His Angels concerning you, to guard you in all your ways.* If you ask why bad things happen, I too do not have an answer for that, but I know when you call God to protect you, He will.

He totally knows you even though you might be a person as ordinary as me, a Filipino by descent, born into a poor family. Oh, by the way, **God chose my race and He chose yours too**. I had no say in that, and I'm cool with it. God has ordained my present, my past and my future's future. When I say my goodbye to the earth, I know I will be with Him in heaven, because I believe in the Word of God (and God's word is flawless) and the Lord Jesus' promise of eternal life for me. All my days are written in the book of life.

You may think, "Why would I need to think of eternal life? I'm very young, free and I'm in good health—I'm just enjoying my life right now." But while you are still young you think of your future, don't you? I remember when I was about nine years old I said to myself, "I wonder where I will be in the year 2,000?" And when you become older or nearer the pension age you will probably have savings, so that you know you will be well off in life here. Wouldn't you think it's also wise to think of your future before you die, so that you're sure to go to heaven, where God wants you to go? You may be thinking, "God knows I would like to go to heaven when I die," or "I am sure I will be there too." Well, the only sure foundation we have while we are on earth is the Word of God. The Lord Jesus Himself said to Nicodemus, *"You must be born again."* You can only be sure your soul will be with the Lord if you have accepted Jesus as your Saviour, Lord and protector of your life, now and for eternity. It's not a hit and miss procedure, it's certain when you make Him as an overseer of your living soul and spirit. You will have the assurance that you will be in heaven with Him.

Do you remember or have you ever read that Cain was hidden away from the presence of God, a vagabond and a restless wanderer, after he killed his brother Abel? Abel's blood was crying out to God for justice because he had been killed unjustly. Justice is established by God, and we will be condemned by the law, the Ten Commandments, that God gave to Moses; but by the grace of the Lord Jesus' death on the Cross we can be saved when we believe in His Word. **God's Word is supreme and always mends people's hearts, and soothes people's souls.**

When Adam and Eve sinned, the Lord God didn't kill them; He clothed them and sent them away from the Garden to stop them carrying on sinning. You know, the minute you know right from wrong, that knowledge which we inherited from Adam and Eve, we became susceptible to bringing judgement on ourselves. You may ask, "Why?" Because we are answerable for our own actions. This is why God didn't stop Cain from killing his brother Abel. God is powerful and He knew the threat Cain was brewing in his heart against his brother. God didn't stop Cain from killing Abel because **God is not willing to violate the freedom He gave to Cain, or to anyone else.** Even though God is so powerful, He is also just and loving. You might think, "Where is the justice on Abel's side?" God knows that though Abel died in the physical he will live again in God's heaven, eternally. Abel was saved from the sinful nature of man on earth before he died. Since it says God was pleased with Abel's sacrifice, he is in God's Kingdom. (He might be one of the 144,000 men who sang a new song in heaven—see Revelation 14:1–5; just a thought.)

God looks at the heart and evaluates the motives of every heart; and the confidence God has in man is found in the condition of his heart. God gave us freewill, to obey Him or to ignore Him, but God always has an answer for all the bad things that happened, and are happening, on earth. God lets all things happen in accordance with His great love for us, so that people may acknowledge their sins and repent. True repentance comes from the heart of a person, and the heart is the centre of God's window to look into every motive in life.

There is always a purpose behind any action; like greed, jealousy, self-exaltation and so on. But what is our main objective or point? We all know what's good and bad, but a lot of people love wrongdoing because they know or think they can get away with it, if the authorities don't catch them. Not so when you're dealing with your conscience before the Lord, and within yourself. Do you think God is not capable of making them good? Of course He is. Do they have the desire to be good and ask God for His help and try to make good choices? I know they don't need to ask God to make themselves bad. Because we are all born sinners, no one is righteous, no—not one; we all fall short of God's glory.

After our ancestors sinned against God, sin encapsulated us, big time. But there is an end to all of this sinning and we need to be reconciled to God, our Maker, so that we can be treated as the Lord Jesus' friend, in heaven. In Luke 16:15, the Lord Jesus was speaking to the Pharisees (who were lovers of money): *He said, "You are those who justify yourselves before men,* **but God**

***knows your hearts**. For what is highly esteemed among men is an abomination in the sight of God."* So God truly knows the heart of everyone.

God looks at the heart, and the Bible says, *For out of the abundance of the heart the mouth speaks*, see Luke 6:45. Where do you catch a fish? In its mouth. And where do you catch a person? In his words. Out of the abundance of the heart the mouth speaks; you might hide it for a while, but eventually it will spill out. In 1 John 3:20, it says: ***If our hearts condemn us, we know that God is greater than our hearts, and He knows everything**.* So repent. That's why forgiveness comes from God, but we need to be honest. Before you speak He knows what you are brewing in your heart, so stop the pretence and let God encourage you to check your heart attitude before Him, and He will release you if you are willing, or allow you to be left alone to the devil's mercy; the only thing is, the devil never knew mercy! But God is merciful and loving, and full of grace. And what is grace? you may ask. It is unmerited favour that we do not deserve, but He gave it anyway because He knows we need it. His grace has no strings attached; He has freely given it to us when we accept and do not refuse God's word (God's Word is His testimony).

There's a song that goes: *Only by grace we can enter, only by grace we can stand, not by human endeavour but by the blood of the Lamb* (the Lord Jesus is known as the Lamb of God). In Isaiah 53:7 it says: *He was oppressed and afflicted, yet he did not open his mouth; he was led like a lamb to the slaughter, and as a sheep before its shearers is silent, so he did not open his mouth*. And in Acts 8:32 this is the passage of Scripture the eunuch was reading: *"He was led like a sheep to the slaughter, and as a lamb before its shearer is silent, so he did not open his mouth."*

This was the grace of carrying all our sins in His own body, dying and rising back to life, by the power of the Holy Spirit, that we may have eternal life through Him. For He carried our own sin and our cross for us.

You might say, "Why would I be included if Jesus carried the Cross and died, and after three days was raised back to life? What has it got to do with me?" Well, let me explain: It is clearly stated and written for your information, *nothing was made that has been made*—in the whole universe—if it wasn't for the Lord Jesus, who was with God, and was God when everything was created in the heavens and on earth. And since you are (alive) on the earth He created, you are under God's authority and power; but because He is very gracious to you He allows you to live on earth. This earth we are inhabiting is His, and for His purpose, and you are included in that purpose because He gave life to you.

So I am fully convinced, more than a hundred percent, that God knows you. All the above passages you have just read are true; *God is not human, that He should lie, not a human being, that He should change His mind. Does He speak and then not act? Does he promise and not fulfil?* (Numbers 23:19).

You do not own your life, you belong to God; and your spirit will return to Him when you die.

2

GOD HAS A PURPOSE FOR YOU

"For I know the plans I have for you," declares the Lord, *"plans to prosper you and not to harm you, plans to give you hope and a future. Then you will call on Me and come and pray to Me, and **I** will listen to you. You will seek Me and find Me when you seek Me with all your heart. I will be found by you,"* declares the Lord (Jeremiah 29:11–14). It also says in Proverbs 3:5 & 6 (instructions and a promise to us): *Trust in the Lord with all your heart, and lean not on your own understanding; in all your ways acknowledge Him, and He shall direct your paths.* These are not just words from the Bible; these are God's instructions, and there is life in God's Words.

You may be thinking, "Why would I have to know and listen to God's Word?" You may be well-off now and be thinking to yourself, "I'm happy with what I've got—I am not a greedy person, I'm contented with my wealth, I don't need God's help; I can do all things." **But remember, your life is borrowed from God**. You might say, "In my plans I will succeed—I'll make sure of it," but remember, you do not hold your life, God does; an illness or an accident can suddenly cut one's life short! And I am not trying to scare you; I'm just mentioning the facts of life.

When you were born God didn't leave you unattended. He has a plan for your existence here on earth, this is what I am talking about. God's plan for your life is always good. Material wealth and goods are God's plan for you too (material wealth is good and it helps you achieve materially), but all worldly wealth will vanish away, though God may prosper you. Did you know that not all wealthy people are happy? Some of them are bound and trapped by their own wealth. Some of them can't sleep well because they're thinking that they need to guard their surroundings just in case some people wanted to get hold of their material wealth. But the wealth I am talking about here is the prosperity of your soul. The wealth that cannot be corrupted or taken away from you; a wealth from Jesus Christ of Nazareth that is hidden in heaven for you, when you make Him your Lord and Saviour. Life on earth is the training ground for our soul to obey God while we are still in our physical bodies on earth. So when our soul and spirit separates from our bodies, we know whom to call. You can certainly have an inner joy when your hope rests in God's goodness, not your own; a hope and joy that money cannot buy; a good relationship with the Lord Jesus that gives you security no matter what is going on in your life today.

You have hope that the peace from God the Father, and joy that only comes from the Lord Jesus, will guide you in life. When you trust God with your life—which He holds, by the way—you can be sure God will do His part to give you hope and a future, prospering you and gifting you; but your part is to seek Him from your heart. Not a wishy washy seeking, but a petition offered to Him in reverence and in truth.

God's plans and purpose for everyone is to know Him, first and foremost. You might ask yourself, "Why does God have to include me with His plan—can't I just be left alone?" We only have two choices: Be in God's plan or be in the devil's chaos; which one would you choose? It's a no-brainer really, isn't it? The fact that God has a better plan for you than your own plan for yourself is a good enough reason to know the Lord Jesus. He knows your future and He knows your past; He holds everything in the palms of His hands. And if you are a believer in Jesus you have a glimpse of knowing this in your mind at least.

The Bible clearly states that no Jew, Greek or even Gentile who is a believer in God's Son is separated from God, for the Lord Jesus accepts anyone and never turns anyone away who comes to Him. John 6:35–40 says: *Then Jesus declared, "I am the bread of life. Whoever comes to Me will never go hungry, and whoever believes in Me will never be thirsty. But as I told you, you have seen Me and still you do not believe. All those the Father gives Me will come to Me, and **whoever comes to Me I will never drive away**. For I have come down from heaven not to do My will but to do the will of Him who sent Me. And this is the will of Him who sent Me; that I shall lose none of all those He has given Me, but raise them up at the last day. **For My Father's will is that everyone who looks to the Son and believes in Him shall have eternal life**, and I will raise them up at the last day."*

So you see, even the Lord Jesus' coming to earth is Father God's plan, to save us all who believe in Him.

You might say that you are not a believer and don't know what to believe. You may think you will be excluded from God's plan and your life has no purpose. Since the Lord created heaven and earth, and you are on earth, then yes, surely God has a plan and purpose for your life. God didn't make the earth inhabited by people He loved just to let them live a meaningless life, just existing on earth and then dying for nothing. And He wasn't lonely in heaven, so that He, you might think, wanted to be praised all the time by people. In fact He is always blasphemed and blamed by people on earth, when bad or even good things happen to them, using His Holy name in vain, which no one should do—as God said in the Ten Commandments: (Exodus 20:7) *"You shall not misuse the name of the Lord your God, **for the Lord will not hold anyone guiltless who misuses His name**.* You never hear anybody blaspheme the names of other gods saying, "For Buddha's sake," or "for Allah's sake," or "for Muhammed's sake, will you stop," no; you don't hear anyone say that, but it's always the Lord's name used as a swear word, or treated with contempt; why? It has become second nature for people to treat God's name as a joke or with contempt; that's truly sad!

Although God chose the Israelites to reveal Himself and His Majesty, He wasn't exclusively just for the Jews. Although Jesus Himself was a Jew, He didn't just die for them but for everyone; He wasn't just good to them alone; for the Lord said, *"He causes the sun to rise on the evil and the good, and sends rain on the righteous and the unrighteous"*(Matthew 5:45). He supplies all your needs (not all your wants).

Does it ever occur to you without the sun and the rain we wouldn't have any food, and there would be no food for the animals either. You couldn't have your favourite chicken, pork, or roast on Sundays. No chocolate, no meringue, no sweets, no crisps, almonds, bread and so on; and as for the vegetarians and vegans—no fruits, no veg., no nuts, no wheat, no cheese, and no milk. Surely God supplies all our needs; He is a good God. He told us these truths so that we may even think of Him as the supplier of our daily living; not just of food, clothing and shelter, but spiritual life too. And we owe gratitude to the Jews who wrote the Word of God for us to read; that we shouldn't have any excuse not to believe God's work and God's Word. The Jews left us the legacy of the historical events in the Holy Scriptures and God gave us all freewill to do good. But a lot of people have rejected God's will because they think they know better; but God knows best.

The knowledge—worldly, natural knowledge—we inherited from the first human beings that corrupted our way not to remain in God's will, made us fall flat at the feet of God, and be dragged along by the enemy because we obeyed him, the liar, the murderer. He told Eve a half truth, that is still a lie. He knows we would be spiritually dead, because he himself died with no sacrifice for his sin, for he was an angel (maybe an overseer of humans) but chose to disobey God. For these fallen angels having died spiritually, only punishment is waiting for them. They knew better than humans do, and I believe there are lots of good and faithful Angels who obey and serve God and do His will.

But for us, God made a way through His Son to re-connect us with Him. Also God the Father made sure there would be a lasting birthday impact on earth for His only Son's birth. God's only Son, Jesus, is the one true citizen of heaven. So Christmas was born and celebrated both in heaven and on earth, where the Archangel was told to tell the whole world about the good news of Jesus' birth. Christmas, the commemoration of His birth, is a day for celebration here on earth as it is also in heaven.

I know that some countries today, like America, have so modernised Christmas and removed the true essence of Christmas from the heart of the celebration. They've watered it down and say, "Happy Holidays" (WHAT IS THEIR HOLIDAY?). I wonder what makes them say that. Perhaps they don't want to offend other religious organisations, or it's not 'politically correct' in their way of thinking to mention Christmas. But they are degrading the 'Birthday Celebrant,' the 'King of all Kings'.

Other religious organisations would stand for what they believe in. A woman I know who is a Buddhist opened her door to a Jehovah's Witness who was telling her about J.W. beliefs and that there is no hell. But she replied and declared loudly, "I'm Buddha!" and shut the door in her face; she didn't care if she offended this soul or not. Some Muslims believers would reprimand Christians for not standing for their own faith—for watering down Christmas greetings. Other religious people are not offended by people saying Happy Christmas; actually, some of them celebrate it too with their family. I worked with some Muslims and Hindus, and I asked them what they do at Christmas time and whether they celebrated that day. They said they commemorate the giving of gifts and being nice to their family, but they don't celebrate Jesus' birthday and they don't recognise Him as the Messiah.

'Happy Christmas' was never offensive to anyone thirty years ago as it seems to be today. I know we have to show respect for other people and not provoke them to anger, but traditional greetings would not show hatred or offend other religious organizations, like the Muslims; but eating pig would offend them. Bad mouthing Muhammed and Allah would cost you your life, but not saying 'Happy Christmas' or 'Happy Easter.' In fact, in my country we call Easter week Holy Week. It's the commemoration of the Holy Son of God—the Sacrificial Lamb—who was slain for the sin of the whole world.

You cannot show what you are standing for if you've lost your spine as a believer in Christ Jesus. Try going to a Muslim country and cooking a whole roast pig in front of them—you'll be dead before you can even slaughter it, let alone cook it. I admire their culture; they truly stand for what they believe in, that Allah is their god. But we have different beliefs from them and we too should stand for what we know is true.

One day every single one of us will stand before God; you and I will be judged by the Lord Jesus. Supposing He asks you about it; what are you going to say in front of Him? He knows your heart before you even utter any word. Would you emphatically say, "It wasn't politically correct, Lord, in my day. I was ashamed of You, and I'm scared of people, so I didn't honour You before them. I belittled You. I did not care what You would think of me because I didn't know that judgement would be coming to all souls. I didn't know I would be judged—no one told me." But today—yes today—I'm telling you, it's all written in the Old and New Testaments, the testimony of God for us.

Remember what the Lord Jesus said when the Pharisees were accusing Him of being the prince of demons? Didn't He say, *'A kingdom divided against itself cannot stand, but if I drive out demons by the finger of God, then the kingdom of God has come upon you,'* see Luke 11:14–20. You might decide to please the people now here on earth, and forget the **one true Celebrant— 'The Son of God,'** where **the celebration begins**; and **with Him it will also end.**

Do you want to modernise the essence of Christmas and refuse to recognise the Birthday Celebrant? Other people don't mind hearing someone say, Merry Christmas! And let me tell you something else, the Lord Jesus said in Mark 8:38: *"**For whoever is ashamed of Me and My Word** in this adulterous and sinful generation, of him **the Son of Man also will be ashamed when He comes in the glory of His Father with the holy angels."*** If you deny Him and His Word, He too will be ashamed of you, to claim you as the co-heir in His Father's Kingdom.

In the two previous verses it says: *"**For what will it profit a man if he gains the whole world and loses his own soul?**"* I don't think you will lose your soul—the enemy will gain it—but where is the respect due to God? Or what will a man give in exchange for his soul? So be very, very, aware that it is the Redeemer, the Saviour of the whole world you are offending. You might say He wouldn't get easily offended, but remember … He is a jealous God.

I am just wondering **why people of other religions are so scared of the Lord Jesus Christ's Name** anyway. I know it's a Sacred Name, it's a powerful Name, and all believers and doers of God's will can lean on His Name. If you do not stand for what you believe in, you will fall, and no one will stand up for your Christian beliefs. And to all those who want to make Jesus known to other people: How could you convince people of different beliefs that you are a believer and follower of Jesus Christ of Nazareth, the Author of life, if you don't stand up in the heart of a democratic country? Where else can you be free to show your true creed? How could one get to know the One true God? If you are not united with other Christian believers then, for you, Christianity will fall. Let it not be.

The Lord's purpose for everyone is that they may seek the Lord in the hope that they may feel for Him and find Him, though He is not far from each one of us, see Acts 17:27. In Isaiah 14:27 it says: **For the Lord of Hosts has purposed and who will annul it?** According to this passage no one can change the purpose of God. And where do we find and read God's purpose? It is written in the Bible. It was the whole Jewish community of faithful (not perfect) believers of God who handed down this legacy of the Holy Scriptures we are enjoying right now. It seems to suggest that the Jews are the executors in the first place and we Christians are participants in letting the other people of different beliefs know the God we know. Romans 8:28–30: *And we know that all things work together for good to those who love God, to those who are the called according to His purpose. For whom He foreknew, He also predestined to be conformed to the image of His Son, that He might be the firstborn among many brethren. Moreover whom He predestined, these He also called;* **whom He called, these He also justified; and whom He justified these He also glorified.**

God never gets it wrong; every detail of our life on earth has been planned by God, but we have a part to play, to step into His plans for us. God gave us choice, but He needs our cooperation. When we get it wrong, God calls to existence the things that do not exist, and He will do that for you too. *Then* **the end will come, when He hands over the kingdom to God the Father** *after He has destroyed all dominion, authority and power,* see 1 Corinthians 15:24. This is God's final victory.

In 1 Corinthians 15:50–57 it says: *Now this I say, brethren, that* **flesh and blood cannot inherit the kingdom of God;** *nor does corruption inherit incorruptible. Behold, I tell you a mystery: We shall not all sleep, but we shall all be changed—in a moment, in the twinkling of an eye, at the last trumpet. For* **the trumpet will sound, and the dead will be raised incorruptible***, and we shall be changed. For this corruptible must put on incorruptible, and this mortal must put on immortality. So when this corruptible has put on incorruptible, and this mortal has put on immortality, then shall be brought to pass the saying that is written: "Death is swallowed up in victory." "O Death, where is your sting? O Hades, where is your victory?" The sting of death* *is sin, and the strength of sin is the law. But thanks be to God, who gives us the victory through our Lord Jesus Christ.*

Isaiah 46:9–11: *Remember the former things of old, for I am God, and there is no other;* ***I am God, and there is none like Me, declaring the end from the beginning****, and from ancient times things that are not yet done, saying, 'My counsel shall stand, and I will do all My pleasure,' calling a bird of prey from the east, the man who executes My counsel, from a far country. Indeed I have spoken it; I will also bring it to pass.* ***I have purposed it; I will also do it.***

Psalm 33:11–13: *The counsel of the Lord stands forever, the plans of His heart to all generations. Blessed is the nation whose God is the Lord, the people He has chosen as His own inheritance. The Lord looks from heaven; He sees all the sons of men.*

Proverbs 18:21: *Death and life are in the power of the tongue and those who love it will eat its fruits.* It means your words have power over you; so speak in a more soberly manner, not pumped up with ill will or idle and boastful words. But say something like, "I am loved by God, and my life is secure in His hands." And if you don't feel well say, "By His wounds I am healed. Holy Spirit release me from this illness."

Do you get what I am saying? If you're a Christian, speak the Word of God over your life and give Him praise, like you're praying; you know praying is just talking from your heart. There's power in prayer and it does change things and circumstances in your life.

Psalm 138:8: **God will fulfil His purpose**.

3

GOD HAS GIFTED YOU

It says in James 1:16–17: *Do not be deceived, my beloved brethren for **every good gift** and **every perfect gift is from above**, and comes down from the Father* (**God**). The gift mentioned here refers to the Lord Jesus, who supplies everything you need. And in Deuteronomy 8:17 & 18: *You may say to yourself, "My power and the strength of my hands have produced this wealth for me."* **But remember the Lord your God, for it is He who gives you the ability to produce wealth.** So therefore it was not you yourself who earned and got all what you have and had, but it was the help of God that gave you strength, good health, and knowledge of the things you are doing, to produce what you are enjoying—your wealth. If you would just remember that your life is borrowed from God, then you can probably say soberly that God has dominion over your entire life, from the time you were born to the time you die. And it's not "Oh poor me, I have to rely on God all my life all the time," but "Yes," because it was He, and He alone, that gave you everything you ever had.

Everything a person owns comes directly or indirectly from God. It is stated here that it wasn't just the strength that we have but also the ability God gave us, and **He imbued in our human flesh our gifts and talents** and everything else, including good health, sound minds and the wisdom we have. The Lord gave King Solomon wisdom beyond and above anyone, and he became well known for this, see 2 Chronicles 1:10–12.

Here are just a few examples of how the Lord gave people the spirit of wisdom in all kinds of artistic design. The Lord gave Bezalel and Oholiab wisdom for making artistic designs on brass and gold and silver, and even on the use of linen of blue, purple and scarlet yarn and embroidery of the embroiderer. God gave the spirit of wisdom to these men. In Exodus 31:1–11 it says: *Then the Lord said to Moses, "See, I have **chosen** Bezalel son of Uri, the son of Hur, of the tribe of Judah, and **I have filled him with the Spirit of God, with wisdom, with understanding, with*** *knowledge and with all kinds of skills* to make artistic designs for work in gold, silver and bronze, to cut and set stones, to work in wood, and to engage in all kinds of crafts. Moreover, I have appointed Oholiab son of Ahisamak, of the tribe of Dan, to help him. Also *I have given ability* to all the skilled workers to make everything I have commanded you: the tent of meeting, the ark of the covenant law with the atonement cover on it, and all the other furnishings of the tent—the table and its articles, the pure gold lampstand and all its accessories, the altar of incense, the altar of burnt offering and all its utensils, the basin with its stand—and also the woven garments, both the sacred garments for Aaron the priest and the garments for his sons when they serve as priests, and the anointing oil and fragrant incense for the Holy Place. They are to make them just as I commanded you." **So God commanded Moses to make the Ark of the Covenant exactly the same as the Ark the Lord God showed Moses when he was on the Mountain of God.** (So it was all God's plan.) And God equipped those men with specific knowledge and wisdom for their job that God assigned for them to do at the command of Moses, God's servant.

So do you think they are better than you? Of course not, without God they wouldn't have these skills.

Everything comes from God. First of all your life, your good health, good understanding, wisdom and knowledge that is unique to you; anything that makes you excel above another in your understanding, but it is not to be so proud of that others could not learn from you. I believe that when the Lord gives wisdom and imparts knowledge to anyone, God will increase what they know so they can impart to someone else what they've learned from Him.

But in this present world a lot of people would think, and you may even think to yourself, "Who needs God? I have everything that I need right now with me. All I want and all I need is at hand—why do I need God to do anything for me when I can do it for myself?" Yes, do what you can and why not, but true Christians need the Holy Spirit's leading in their hearts every day. I myself say this: that not because I can talk, walk, think and put into action what I need to do, that I don't need the Holy Spirit—but I do; I still badly need the Holy Spirit in my life every day. I don't have inner joy and inner peace without the knowledge and the presence of the Holy Spirit in me every day.

You might ask, "Every day?" Yes, you need Him every day! It's like, you ... you know you don't need your mum or your dad to take your hand to walk or to eat, or whatever you can physically do every day, do you? But at the back of your mind (and this is if you have normal parents) you know you always need them; just the knowledge that they love you and that they are always on your side means that you can count on them as people you can associate with, respect and love as much as they love you, knowing you belong to them because they are your natural parents. But God the Father loves you more than any human has ever loved you.

When you have already accepted the Lord Jesus as your Saviour, and you still feel there's something missing in you, and you can't quite think what's lacking or missing in your deeper soul, then I could only say: this is the time you need the Holy Spirit of God in you.

You know in Matthew 25:1–13, the parable of the five wise virgins and the five foolish ones? They all had lamps but the five foolish ones didn't have oil with them when the bridegroom arrived. For us it means we need the Holy Spirit to guide and lead us, to keep the fervour of God in our everyday lives and be ready for when the Lord returns. And we need to seek the fellowship of the Holy Spirit so we can walk in humbleness of heart every day. We cannot keep our hearts pure without the guidance of the Holy Spirit, that's why the Lord Jesus promised His disciples the coming of the Holy Spirit to replace the physical, visible presence of the Lord Jesus in their midst. He instructed them to wait for the Holy Spirit to come upon them, with the promise they would receive power. So if the Lord Jesus told His disciples the Holy Spirit was necessary for them to have, we too need the Holy Spirit's presence and power over us. It's like this: your spirit was slumbering before you accepted the Lord Jesus, but was awakened when you accepted Him, right? So we need perpetual guidance of the Holy Spirit in our everyday lives, to enlighten and empower us through God's Word, speaking to our spirit man and soul that have been awakened by the Spirit of the Living God, ok?

The Holy Spirit is the One that's lacking in some Christians' lives. When the leading and the guidance and the fellowship of the Holy Spirit is lacking in one's soul, that is when you would normally feel empty or incomplete. If you don't want your heart feeling empty and dissatisfied, then do this: Place your hand on your heart and say:

"Precious God the Holy Spirit, help me. I'm accepting You in my heart, and I'm inviting You to cleanse me. I welcome You, that You may sit on the throne of my heart and be my guide forever; lead me please and guard my heart that I may not sin against You. Hear my prayer, O God; in Jesus' name I ask this, Amen."

And when you wake up in the morning; say, "Good Morning Holy Spirit," and again invite Him in your heart to be with you all day, and feel and see the difference it will bring to your life. I can assure you, you will feel the inner joy and peace of heart and mind from Him, if you mean what you say. The only thing that might hinder you from receiving Him is your mind-set. So renew your mind by believing in Him and even ask Him to help you renew your mind. Say "Lord God the Holy Spirit, help me to have the mind of Christ in me, Amen."

If you have not accepted the Lord as your Saviour yet, then place your hand on your heart and say this simple prayer: "Lord Jesus, forgive me for all the sins that I've ever done in my life; I turn my back away from all of these sins I have committed (name the sins you really know are wrong, even if it is swearing, or thinking bad about other people or anything like hatred you're holding in your heart against anyone). I'm sorry, Lord, for everything I've done wrong."

And if you remember other people who have done wrong to you say: "I forgive them, Lord; please, Lord, help me erase all my pain, I set him or her (name them) free. I put all my pain at the foot of Your Cross. Set them free, O Lord; I forgive them, that You may forgive me too, and set me free too from all things that are hindering me from knowing Your peace and knowing You from my heart and my soul. Lord, O Lord, liberate me. I accept You as my personal Saviour and protector and the Lord of my life." Then say, "Holy Spirit, I accept You to be my Lord and guide forever, in the Name of Jesus, Amen." Close your eyes and spend a few minutes just waiting for the Holy Spirit to respond to your request, leaving your hand on your heart.

If you didn't feel the Holy Spirit, then go back and re-read and follow those simple instructions and you will notice the change in your everyday life for the good of your own soul. You know what? We love checking things to see if they really work, don't we? And I know that if you mean what you are saying to the Holy Spirit (the Central Power) of God, you will experience God's Holy Presence in your life.

Some people may think when you die that's it—you're dead and nothing of you remains—but according to what I've read in Mathew 24:35 (the Lord Jesus speaking): *Heaven and earth will pass away* **but My words** *will by no means pass away.* I suppose I want you to be aware that heaven is made for the resting place of our soul and spirit, and the best assurance we have is knowing that the Lord Jesus died on the Cross for all people (whether you know it or not), extending His grace in rescuing humanity from hell.

I have three examples here that the death of a man is *not* the complete finish of his life:

1. Luke 16:19–31: (The Lord Jesus Himself speaking in these passages): *"There was a rich man who was dressed in purple and fine linen and lived in luxury every day. At his gate was laid a beggar named Lazarus, covered with sores and longing to eat what fell from the rich man's table. Even the dogs came and licked his sores.*

"The time came when the beggar died and the angels carried him to Abraham's side. The rich man also died and was buried. In Hades, where he was in torment, he looked up and saw Abraham far away, with Lazarus by his side. So he called to him, 'Father Abraham, have pity on me and send Lazarus to dip the tip of his finger in water and cool my tongue, because I am in agony in this fire.'

"But Abraham replied, 'Son, remember that in your lifetime you received your good things, while Lazarus received bad things, but now he is comforted here and you are in agony. And

GOD'S INVITATION FOR YOU AWAITS

besides all this, between us and you a great chasm has been set in place, so that those who want to go from here to you cannot, nor can anyone cross over from there to us.'

"He answered, 'Then I beg you, father, send Lazarus to my family, for I have five brothers. Let him warn them, so that they will not also come to this place of torment.'

"Abraham replied, 'They have Moses and the Prophets; let them listen to them.'

"'No, father Abraham,' he said, 'but if someone from the dead goes to them, they will repent.'

"He said to him, 'If they do not listen to Moses and the Prophets, they will not be convinced even if someone rises from the dead.'"

There was One that rose from the dead, His name is Jesus and His testimony is perfect. God the Father sent Him, and He was the one speaking those words.

What I am saying here is, luxury and wealth are not bad, and you will not go to hell because you are rich, but what I am trying to explain and show you here is, this rich man had no compassion on Lazarus, and even with them being both dead he still expected Lazarus to do something for him because he still remembered that he was poor here on earth, but he didn't even own Lazarus as his slave, or even treat Lazarus' sores. The dogs had more compassion on Lazarus than this rich man mentioned here.

So if you have a chance to be compassionate for the Lazarus of your time, do so, so that money and pride and self-exaltation should not have a hold on you. This rich man the Lord Jesus spoke of had his material wealth get hold of him. Twinned with pride and uncompassionate self-absorption, that became the downfall of him—down to hell.

Why do you think the Lord Jesus mentioned hell in front of all who listened to Him? I suppose just to let them, and us, know about it. Surely the rich man could have made Lazarus one of his yard sweepers and he could have had his left-overs, but he hardened his heart towards this beggar.

God is not against people gaining wealth, that's why he gave people ability to produce wealth. You see, God made King Solomon very rich and Job too—so that he accumulated twice as much as he had before he was tested. So what I am trying to say here is God is not against wealth and money, but the *love* of money and the pride of life became the source of evil to this rich man.

2. The Lord Jesus Himself was raised back to life on the third day, by God the Father through the redeeming Power of the Holy Spirit, and He walked on earth for forty days before His ascension and **He promised to be back again to claim the souls** (it is the soul that feels the pain) **of all mankind who believe in Him**. He was sent by Father God in the first place to resurrect those who would believe in Him. But those who do not believe, He said they are condemned already.

What is my point of telling you this? It's to let you know that Jesus Christ is the God of all the living (you're alive because of your spirit) and souls of mankind, and the Lord Jesus mentioned that Abraham, Isaac and Jacob, though they died long ago, are alive spiritually. In Matthew 22:29–32: *Jesus replied, "You are in error because you do not know the Scriptures or the power of God. At the resurrection people will neither marry nor be given in marriage; they will be like the angels in heaven. But about the resurrection of the dead—have you not read what God said to you, 'I am the God of Abraham, the God of Isaac, and the God of Jacob'?* ***He is not the God of the dead but of the living.****" When the crowds heard this, they were astonished at his teaching* (see also Luke 20:27–38).

All I know is, the Lord Jesus is coming back and He wants you to wait for His return, His second coming, when He will judge those spirits who completely rejected Him as a Son of God.

These events in the Bible are the witness of His disciples and the Lord Jesus' very own Testimony to the world, that what had happened to Him and through Him and all that He was saying in His Word, are truly going to happen. His return is now becoming imminent, and **God does not want any human in hell**, but **God wants us all in heaven**; that's why He sent His Son to pay the penalty for our sins. No human apart from God's own Son had the power to disarm the enemy, and He has already overcome the power of the enemy. Only God's own Son could do this, for He alone was born sinless.

You may ask how I could say this. It's because He was conceived through the Word of God by God's own Spirit, the Holy Spirit, which came upon Mary His Mother for Him to enter a sinful world. He was born by a human being, Mary, by the Spirit of God; so a human mingled with God, fused together. That's how He could rescue us; we need collaboration with God, not with the enemy.

Before the devil became a devil, he could differentiate good from evil—he was an Angel of God, higher than human beings, who were created from the dust of the ground. Because the devil had a power almost like God, so he thought, but definitely far below than that of the Lord Jesus who was the Word of God, it's like there's no competition—the devil will always lose.

But the devil could accuse the Lord Jesus that their fight is not equal. The Lord Jesus had already got more power than the devil so God made a solution that He, the Word—the Lord Jesus Himself—would be born of woman in a human form, as Adam and Eve were in a human form. So the devil could not taunt the Lord by saying "But you are God" He made Himself into a human to live under the human law, the law of the land, if you get what I mean, to rescue us humans. It's like the devil was the reason that the cord was cut off between God and the man He created; but so that we can be connected again to God we have to choose His Son as our Lord, and King and Saviour, to become alive spiritually. When you are not acknowledging Jesus as your Saviour, though alive physically your spirit is slumbering spiritually, and needs to be awakened by God the Holy Spirit within you.

We didn't witness when Adam and Eve sinned but we believe the written account because it was the breath of God—His Word is His breath. But the breath that God breathed into Adam and Eve is the spirit breath that made them alive. That breath of God in us, which is the spirit of man, is the spirit that will return to God when we die, if we believe the Father God's Word. It was, and is, God's legacy to humanity. So our spirit can only go back to God if we invest back our spirits in the Only Son of God who died for us.

If you don't believe, you are condemned already. But there is still time to believe, and if you think everything you read in here is just gobbledygook, nonsense, **then why would God leave the Bible as a legacy, if it was just to tell all people about nonsense**? No point. Why would the Lord Jesus, who suffered so much in the eyes of humanity (watch the Passion of the Christ movie), tell those who killed Him, "Forgive them Father for they know not what they are doing ..." Why would the Lord Jesus ask Father God to forgive those people who killed Him? What is the point of forgiveness? Surely it did not originate from man but from God.

We also didn't witness when the Lord Jesus actually died for us on the Cross, but we (or I) believe it was the conviction of our spirit—and every spirit is far stronger than the flesh.

If you don't believe in the written Word, the Bible, it's like reading all the history of a certain country and just saying that it is all nonsense, it never happened; when you really should be getting information from the past generations that were here before you. You can't really argue that it wasn't Christopher Columbus who discovered America; you cannot say, "Oh no, no, no way; it was Tony Smith!" A lot of people try to disprove the Bible writings, and try to invalidate the stories in them. They might accept the wars and other history in them, and may even believe in The Ten Commandments, but they (or a lot of people) don't accept the Lord Jesus' death as a sacrifice for them, to save their soul from the pit of hell.

It is stated clearly that only Jesus has all the Right of Payment for our sins, although it wasn't Him who sinned but us, all humanity. He paid for us! He was sinless but died for *our* sins.

Only the Lord Jesus is more than equal in power and strength to the devil, who deceived Eve and Adam in the Garden of Eden. This is where the first sin started, because the devil was in the Garden and that's why he managed to deceive the woman.

Would you believe that the devil who deceived Eve in the Garden of Eden was an Angel of God? He was a covering Angel who walked among the fiery coals and was perfect in beauty, but he became proud and trampled on God's Holiness, so he was cast down to the ground and became the lowest of the low after he had enticed Eve and deceived her so she and Adam would disobey God's instruction.

3. Luke 20:27–38: *Then **some of the Sadducees, who deny that there is a resurrection**, came to Him* (the Lord Jesus) *and asked Him, saying: "Teacher, Moses wrote to us that if a man's brother dies, having a wife, and he dies without children, his brother should take his wife and raise up offspring for his brother. Now there were seven brothers. And the first took a wife, and died without children. And the second took her as wife, and he died childless. Then the third took her, and in like manner the seven also; and they left no children, and died. Last of all, the woman died also. **Therefore, in the resurrection*** (why would the resurrection be mentioned, if when we die that's it; we're finished?), *whose wife does she become? For all seven had her as wife."*

*Jesus answered and said to them, "The sons of this age marry and are given in marriage. But those who are **counted worthy to attain that age, and the resurrection from the dead**, neither marry nor are given in marriage; **nor can they die anymore**, for **they are equal to the angels and are sons of God**, being sons of the resurrection. But even Moses showed in the burning bush passage that the dead are raised, when he called the Lord **'the God of Abraham, the God of Isaac, and the God of Jacob.' For He is not the God of the dead but of the living, for all live through Him."***

Jesus' disciples saw two of those who died long ago when the Lord Jesus was with Peter and John on the Mountain of Olives. Moses and Elijah appeared to them talking to the Lord Jesus. They saw them so alive that *Peter said to Jesus, "Lord, it is good for us to be here. If you wish, I will put up three shelters—one for You, one for Moses and one for Elijah"* (Matthew 17:4). (See also Mark 9:5 and Luke 9:33.) This Moses, the man of God, and Elijah, the prophet of God, were walking and living on earth, way back in Old Testament times; but Peter and John weren't born then. Moses died and God buried him, in a valley in the land of Moab—but to this day no one really knows where his grave is (see Deuteronomy 34:6)—and Elijah was taken up to heaven by God in a chariot of fire, see 2 Kings 2:11.

Have you ever wondered why Peter and John recognised Moses and Elijah talking to the Lord Jesus? And you may even ask how comes the Lord Jesus knows them, if we are thinking soberly with just head knowledge? Because Moses and Elijah were a long time gone, unseen on earth. If I've remembered it well (taken from the internet), Moses was born in 1525 B.C. while Elijah began his ministry in 870 B.C. and his birth was not recorded. While the Lord Jesus was born of Mary about 2018 years ago (the year we are using is the year of His birth).

Do you feel intrigued or amazed at what John the Baptist said when he was testifying concerning the Lord Jesus? Jesus was here and was the executer of the Word of God before even John the Baptist was born; but the Lord Jesus was actually born on earth six months after the birth of John the Baptist, so he was six months younger than him. And John also said he was not worthy to stoop down and untie the Lord Jesus' sandals. When John the Baptist sent his own disciples to the Lord Jesus and asked who He was, *"Are You the One who is to come or shall I expect somebody else?"* the Lord Jesus replied, *"The lame walk, the blind see, and the Gospel is preached to the poor."* So John knew this was his time to elevate the Lord Jesus in His place.

I could see the Lord Jesus was saying to the Sadducees that Abraham, Isaac, and Jacob are still alive (Abraham was buried in Machpelah in Hebron, as was his son Isaac, but Jacob was buried in Canaan) and their spirits carry on living. Though they are already physically dead and will not return to earth ever again, they are in fact alive and living in the place where God put them to exist.

No amount of your own sacrifice, not even material wealth, can make you feel free of your wrongdoing except the redeeming blood of the Lord Jesus and the work of the Holy Spirit of God in your life. Your material wealth is useless in heaven; you cannot buy anything there—no transactions or bartering or exchange take place in heaven. **The exchange took place at the Cross of Calvary in Golgotha—here on earth, when Jesus died for our sins, and then after three days rose again.**

Every living person has a spirit, and your spirit will live forever—**you don't die and that's it.** You have the choice of everlasting life with the Lord Jesus or everlasting torment in hell. Now that I have explained all these things **you cannot say** that

there's no hell, because even **the Lord Jesus** Himself **mentioned it.** (See Luke 16:23.)

If you have never done the exchange yet (it's just words, but with sincerity of your heart, that would make the exchange), while you have breath in your nostrils you still have a chance to accept the Lord Jesus as your Lord and Saviour here on earth, so that you have security in receiving **God's gift** of eternal life in heaven (like getting eternal life insurance while you're still alive, and not when you're already dead, because it's too late).

No amount of persuasion in your own mind can erase a guilty charge over you that the enemy could accuse you of when you are already dead and standing before the throne of God to be judged. Oh, what a frightening thought! So while you are still alive get the Lord Jesus on your side to agree with you; have Him as your Lord and Saviour, do it while you are on earth while your spirit is still inside your physical body. And you cannot exchange any of your material wealth for the redemption of your spirit and soul. Your feeling of guilt will remain in your mind and memory, unless the Spirit of the Living God (the Holy Spirit) cleanse and clear your own conscience.

Whether we acknowledge it or not, the reality is God gifted us all with wisdom; and if the wisdom you have is not enough for the task you are planning to do, ask God; for He says He gives liberally without finding fault and it will be given to you. It simply means that you ask with all of your heart and God will give it to you. (King Solomon asked for wisdom and God gave him extra ordinary wisdom.) It says in James 1:5: *If anyone of you lacks wisdom, ask God and it will be given to you.*

And you cannot have anything without the Lord's provision for you. When you hear someone say, "That person is gifted," his or her ability, ingenuity and talents come from God alone. We can study and learn more about the things we do not know yet, or are not familiar with; that's why it says in the physical sense to get wisdom and understanding even if it cost you all your wealth, see Proverbs 4:7. That's why we go to college and university to increase our knowledge, to observe and study, but there is a supernatural knowledge that only God can give, like spiritual Godly knowledge. Not everyone has it because it is gifted to us by God. We have all different kinds of wisdom inborn in us: some blind people who cannot read musical notes can play the piano perfectly well by listening—they have the gift of good hearing and wisdom to apply what they envisage. The gift God gave us enabled us to excel not just in knowledge and wisdom, but also in material wealth.

Yes, you can buy everything here on earth—gold, jewels, cars, houses, mansions, yachts, aeroplanes; everything that money can buy you can have—as long as it is available to you. But all material things will perish in time.

And we know in heaven there are no transactions, and I'm telling you, the streets of heaven are paved with gold, and the water there is flowing with life and peace.

The Lord's gift for you is your license to excel in everything you do, and it is necessary for your everyday life. And as I've previously mentioned, remember God—for it is He who gives you the ability to produce wealth.

God doesn't want you to be poor, He doesn't want you just to strive in life, He wants you to be successful.

4

GOD CREATED THE WORLD AROUND YOU

Before God created any man on earth, He made sure there would be a place of lasting ordinance—between God and man. First of all, He created the heavens and the earth, the day and the night, the stars and everything from heaven that gave light on earth. Then God separated the water above the sky from the water below. At that time there was no rain, but mist watered the surface of the ground. Then God made everything that swims in the sea and He also made all the creatures that walk and creep along the ground. Then He made this beautiful garden that was absolutely perfect, with friendly living creatures of all kinds. There were all types of birds flying to and fro in the sky above, singing as the morning stars rose. Has it ever occurred to you that the stars in the galaxy praise God in the morning as the new day comes?

There were fishes of magnificent colours glinting in the deep blue seas as they swam. On earth the cattle were grazing in the lush meadows, living peacefully with lions and tigers—without fear of being pursued by them. (This was before any human being sinned.) The magnificence of the sun shining brightly across the cloudless sky was reflected on the lakes, with the cool breeze blowing swiftly through the trees making them sway back and forth. The serenity of the whole place was being transformed at every angle into a vivid unimaginable scene; it was varied and totally breath-taking. This place was surrounded with all species of plants with diverse colours, shapes, sizes and scents, and fruit-bearing trees that served as food for all the created living things.

God made all sorts of wild animals, livestock and small animals, each able to reproduce more of its own kind, and God saw it was very good (Genesis 1:25). And God decided He'd have someone to look after His creation, and out of the dust of the earth, he moulded a man. God breathed on Adam the breath of life, and he became a living being.

Adam was created in the image of God (Genesis 1:26). He

wasn't created as a robot that would follow everything he had been commanded to do. God loved him and gave him free will. God gave him a definite superiority among every living creature to rule over them and subdue them, from the birds of the air, to the fish of the sea, to everything that walks and moves and creeps on the ground.

Now the Lord God had formed out of the ground all the beasts and all the birds of the air. He brought them to the man to see what he would name them; and whatever the man called each living creature, that was its name (Genesis 2:19). (I believe that the names Adam gave to these creatures remain today.) God gave him power over them, with supernatural wisdom and an excellent foreknowledge. He became superior among every created living thing on earth.

There was no barrier between God and Adam; he communicated with God and had fellowship with Him. He stood where God stood and walked where God walked. Everything he needed was at hand and there was no shortage of anything in his life. And there was no law to follow straight away, just the instruction to name the animals and what not to do (do not eat from the tree…). Freedom and fellowship is what Adam had with God. He was hard working, and didn't moan, and he was obedient to God. And God was concerned about his welfare too. Adam had so much to do, and God saw that he needed a helper, some company.

Animals communicated with animals, but Adam had no one to talk to. Among other creatures God made, there was no equal, so God caused him to fall deeply asleep and took part of his rib to create a woman. It makes me think: **Why would the woman be taken out of the man's rib and not from the ground, like the man** and any other living thing? Just a thought … maybe Adam would treat her like an animal if God had formed Eve out of the ground. But because she was taken and made from the man's rib she was loved and treated as himself, equal to him. Only after she was created did God give them a specific command. He blessed them and commanded them to be fruitful and increase in number (Adam could not reproduce on his own), to fill the earth and subdue it. The purpose, I believe, was to communicate with each other their thoughts and feelings, to express themselves with each other and have a relational fellowship.

From the beginning God created marriage between man and woman. Reproduction was introduced first to the animals, birds of the air and fish of the sea and then to humans; so family life began. Yet it didn't actually start until the fall of man, as we know it—or did it? We don't know if they had children in the Garden, yet they wouldn't be natural beings like us. That's what I believe. So maybe when God said, "Be fruitful and multiply," perhaps He could see Eve's hand on that tree of the knowledge of good and evil. Or did they reproduce before the fall?

As I know, when God speaks out of His Word, things exist. But not in the ordinary way we know of, otherwise the Garden of Eden would have been defiled by a trail of blood from Eve, every month. Again, I believe after the Lord punished the woman, her period started; because God said to her, *"I will greatly multiply your sorrow and your conception; in pain you will bring forth children; your desire will be for your husband, and he shall rule over you"* (Genesis 3:16).

The Garden of Eden was their perfect and free-of-sin abode. We don't know for how long they had lived there; maybe hundreds, maybe thousands of years, before the crafty snake appeared and asked a question that made the woman think, *"Did God really say, 'You must not eat from any tree in the garden'?"* (Genesis 3:1). You see, the serpent could speak then. He awoke the woman's imagination and said, *"You will not surely die* (he convinced Eve); *for God knows **when you eat of it** your eyes will be opened, and you will be like God knowing good and evil"* (verses 4 & 5). The devil told Eve half the truth. It's true, they did not drop dead in the garden; and her mind was straight away receptive towards knowledge. She thought she would be like God! Wow—knowing good and evil! What they did not know was it was spiritual death, a physical separation of man from God. Their spiritual senses died, or maybe were detained in a comatose realm or state; they could then only see in the physical—fleshly objects, and whatever God intended them to see at that time.

I believe the serpent knew he could not tempt Adam because he got the instruction directly from God's mouth, so the devil waited for the opportunity to come. And I believe the fallen angel, the deceiver, sinned before any human being ever did, otherwise he could never have deceived Eve. That devil wanted the whole human creation to disappoint God. So he truly waited for that opportunity to deceive the woman who was weak yet decisive. So the very first sin was committed.

I was wondering ... there were two trees in the middle of the garden: **the tree of life** and **the tree of the knowledge of good and evil**. Why did the devil insist on saying to Eve, or entice her, to eat from the tree of the knowledge of good and evil and not from the tree of life, and say to her, "You will live forever"?

As they were already living as spiritual beings at that time, sinning never entered their mind—no guilt trip in their conscience, and they were not brainless; they really were full of wisdom and knowledge of God, not of evil. I believe they didn't know evil then, since they were crafted by God as innocent beings. They only became human living beings after God breathed on them the breath of life. **The breath of life that God breathed on Adam's and Eve's nostrils from Him is the spirit of man.**

I do believe the enemy wanted us humans to side with him; he hated that God always had a power above him. But then God gave *us* power above him when the Lord God said, *"You will crush his head, and he will strike your heel"*—we could stamp him out underfoot. I believe these devils (the fallen angels as they were) were also created in God's image, although it isn't stated that way in the Bible. But **I've seen an Angel** (a good Angel), and **he looks like an ordinary human being**. They are supernatural beings—servants of God. Yet God could make anyone unrecognisable to everybody if God wishes to, because on the very day the Lord Jesus was resurrected from the dead, two of Jesus' disciples, who were walking on their way to Emmaus, didn't recognise Him. Only after He gave thanks and broke bread with them and disappeared in front of them did they realise He was the Risen Christ, see Luke 24:13–35. And I think every time the enemy sees us, he's looking at the power above him after the fall of man. The devil probably wasn't aware of it before God punished him. He didn't know what was coming to him!

The devil wasn't threatened that humans would fall out with him. In fact he thought we would forever submit to him when Adam and Eve, or we even in today's life, ignored God.

Before the Lord Jesus came, the devil thought he had won when we disobeyed God; but not so, for after Jesus' death we were redeemed by the power of His blood and grace. The Lord Jesus' sacrificial death purchased back our eternal life for us, when we believe in Him and receive Him as our Saviour. And if you want eternal life in heaven with Him, it is not optional to accept Jesus as the Only Saviour who could testify of His grace and has erased the devil's claim for your soul.

But the devil was losing his battle with God the minute God had the tree of life guarded by the cherubim with the sword that was flashing back and forth to guard the way to the tree of life. Because God the Father then knew He would send His One and Only Son and bring us back for Himself. Since the deceiver was punished to walk on its belly for the rest of its life and that the woman would crush its head, it means he was put down lower than human beings in God's sight (**you can only crush the head of someone or something that is below you**).

Before the temptation, the woman did not know how to choose between good and bad; the only thing she ever knew was *good* at that time before she was tempted. It's not that she didn't have a choice; it's just it never entered her mind before she fell for the snake's idea. But now we have no choice because sin was handed down to us by human descent—the first sinners being Adam and Eve. They simply didn't know how to disobey God before the temptations. You may be saying, "I thought you said they were given an extraordinary foreknowledge?" Yes, above every animal, bird and fish, but not above the Angels—they probably never even saw the Angels of God that weren't the fallen ones. And how would they ever distinguish the fallen angels from the obedient ones, because they simply didn't know *good* from *bad*?

Everything belongs to God. And do you think you'd be better off without knowing what you know now? We were conceived through sin; it started when Adam and Eve were thrown out of the garden. The minute sin entered into the world through the first man's disobedience, indeed we multiplied. The man became the authority and the head of the family. Even in that beginning God said to the woman her desire would be for her husband and he would rule over her. (If both husband and wife are Christians the husband is the sort of covering over the wife, and he has to have the authority over her.) There is one passage in Scripture that says if the wife has made a vow and the husband does not revoke it her vow stands, but if the husband forbids her to make that vow, then her vow is without meaning—it's revoked in the sight of God. Or if the unmarried daughter who is still living in her father's house made a vow and the father heard it and he did not say anything when she made that vow, then her vow still stands; but if her father rebuked or forbade her to do so, her vow will be revoked, see Numbers 30:1–16.

I've just read that even in the Islamic laws, if the husband disallows his wife to make a vow, her vow will not be valid. Can you see the power and the authority the Lord God put onto the shoulders of a man, as a father or as a husband?

I also believe that God tests His people to reveal to them He is the Creator and to show them His Omnipotence. In Deuteronomy 13:3 it says: *For the Lord your God is testing you, to know whether you love the Lord your God with all your heart and with all your soul.* **God withdrew from Hezekiah in order to test him**, so that God might know all that was in Hezekiah's heart. (See 2 Chronicles 32:30–31.) God is longing to see if a person will obey him wholeheartedly (a choice) and for how long. I also realise, reading Luke 22:31–32, that God does talk to His adversary. When the devil told the Lord Jesus to sift Simon, Jesus disagreed with him, for only the Lord Jesus knows the condition of a man's heart and spirit, for the Lord lived and mingled with mankind and knew His people's strength. And sometimes God allows an adversary to test us ... see the book of Job. But God also rebukes the enemy, see Zechariah 3:1–2.

The Lord tests people and He is not scared that people might fail, because God looks at the integrity of people's heart towards Him. At the enemy's insistence the Lord tested Job, and after the testing came the strengthening from Him.

Let me tell you about the background of the servant of God named Job. He was a wealthy man from Uz; a man who feared God and shunned evil. A well-respected man in his home town, he had seven sons and three daughters, and he owned seven thousand sheep, three thousand camels, five hundred yoke of oxen and five hundred female donkeys, and had a large number of servants; and he was one of the wealthiest men in his time. His sons in turn would have a feast in their homes and invite their three sisters to eat and drink with them.

When the day of feasting was over, Job would send and sanctify them and he would rise early the next morning and offer burnt offerings according to the number of them all. For Job said, *"It may be that my sons have sinned and cursed God in their hearts."* This was Job's regular custom.

Now there was a day when the sons of God came to present themselves before the Lord, and Satan also came among them. And the Lord said to Satan, "From where do you come?" So Satan answered the Lord and said, "From going to and fro on the earth, and from walking back and forth on it." (The Lord knows that Satan got redundant for a while, for no one truly bothered to seek God on earth, apart from Job, and maybe a few other people.) *Then the Lord said to Satan, "Have you considered My servant Job, that there is none like him on the earth, a blameless and upright man, one who fears God and shuns evil?"*

So Satan answered the Lord and said, "Does Job fear God for nothing? Have You not made a hedge around him, around his household, and around all that he has on every side? You have blessed the work of his hands, and his possessions have increased in the land. But now, stretch out Your hand and touch all that he has, and he will surely curse You to Your face!"

And the Lord said to Satan, "Behold, all that he has is in your power; only do not lay a hand on his person" (Job 1:6–12).

So the Lord God allowed the enemy to test Job but He warned him not to touch Job's life. As a result all Job's possessions vanished in a matter of days and even his ten children died and he was tormented emotionally and physically; even his friends contended with him, accusing him of wrong doing. His own wife told him to curse God and die; his own breath was offensive to his wife's nostrils and he was unrecognisable by his own friends. But as they were contending, Job held on to his integrity. He didn't accuse God of wrongdoing; in fact he said, *"Naked I come and naked I will depart, the Lord gave and the Lord has taken away."* But still three of his friends discoursed with him and found Job speaking as if he were right in his own eyes. Yet in front of his friends he maintained his own integrity. But the young man Elihu condemned Job self-righteousness, until God revealed His Omnipotence to Job. Job wanted God to speak to him, so **the Lord spoke to Job** and asked him a question and told Job all the things he didn't know—and for us to know, **so we should know what God has done for us** and to understand that **God is the ultimate Creator of everything.**

Here in Job 39 **God questions Job**: *"Do you know when the mountain goats give birth? Do you watch when the doe bears her fawn? Do you count the months till they bear? Do you know the time they give birth? They crouch down and bring forth their young; their labour pains are ended. Their young thrive and grow strong in the wilds; they leave and do not return.*

"Who let the wild donkey go free, who untied its ropes? I gave it the wasteland as its home, the salt flats as its habitat. It laughs at the commotion in the town; it does not hear a driver's shout.

It ranges the hills for its pasture and searches for any green thing.

"Will the wild ox consent to serve you? Will it stay by your manger at night? Can you hold it to the furrow with a harness? Will it till the valleys behind you? Will you rely on it for its great strength? Will you leave your heavy work to it? Can you trust it to haul in your grain and bring it to your threshing floor?

"The wings of the ostrich flap joyfully, though they cannot compare with the wings and feathers of the stork. She lays her eggs on the ground and lets them warm in the sand, un-mindful that a foot may crush them, that some wild animal may trample them. She treats her young harshly, as if they were not hers; she cares not that her labour was in vain, for God did not endow her with wisdom or give her a share of good sense. Yet when she spreads her feathers to run, she laughs at horse and rider.

"Do you give the horse its strength or clothe its neck with a flowing mane? Do you make it leap like a locust, striking terror with its proud snorting? It paws fiercely, rejoicing in its strength,

and charges into the fray. It laughs at fear, afraid of nothing; it does not shy away from the sword. The quiver rattles against its side, along with the flashing spear and lance. In frenzied excitement it eats up the ground; it cannot stand still when the trumpet sounds. At the blast of the trumpet it snorts, 'Aha!' It catches the scent of battle from afar, the shout of commanders and the battle cry.

"Does the hawk take flight by your wisdom and spread its wings toward the south? Does the eagle soar at your command and build its nest on high? It dwells on a cliff and stays there at night; a rocky crag is its stronghold. From there it looks for food; its eyes detect it from afar. Its young ones feast on blood, and where the slain are, there it is."

Job 40: *The Lord said to Job:* "*Will the one who contends with the Almighty correct him? Let him who accuses God answer him!"* **Then Job answered the Lord**: *"I am unworthy—how can I reply to you?*

I put my hand over my mouth. I spoke once, but I have no answer—twice, but I will say no more."

Then the Lord spoke to Job out of the storm: "Brace yourself like a man; I will question you, and you shall answer me.

"Would you discredit my justice, would you condemn me to justify yourself? Do you have an arm like God's, and can your voice thunder like His? Then adorn yourself with glory and splendour, and clothe yourself in honour and majesty. Unleash the fury of your wrath, look at all who are proud and bring them low, look at all who are proud and humble them, crush the wicked where they stand. Bury them all in the dust together; shroud their faces in the grave. Then I myself will admit to you that your own right hand can save you.

"Look at Behemoth, which I made along with you and which feeds on grass like an ox. What strength it has in its loins, what power in the muscles of its belly! Its tail sways like a cedar; the sinews of its thighs are close-knit. Its bones are tubes of bronze, its limbs like rods of iron. It ranks first among the works of God, yet its Maker can approach it with his sword. The hills bring it their produce, and all the wild animals play nearby. Under the lotus plants it lies, hidden among the reeds in the marsh. The lotuses conceal it in their shadows the poplars by the stream

surround it. *A raging river does not alarm it; it is secure, though the Jordan should surge against its mouth. Can anyone capture it by the eyes, or trap it and pierce its nose?*

God showed Job His authority over His creation. Job was dumbfounded, and put his hand over his mouth, seeing that what the Lord described to him is the work of His own hands. Then God prospered Job after his time of testing was over.

And everything the Lord created has a season of its own:

There is a time for everything, and a season for every activity under the heavens: a time to be born and a time to die, a time to plant and a time to uproot, a time to kill and a time to heal, a time to tear down and a time to build, a time to weep and a time to laugh, a time to mourn and a time to dance, a time to scatter stones and a time to gather them, a time to embrace and a time to refrain from embracing, a time to search and a time to give up, a time to keep and a time to throw away, a time to tear and a time to mend, a time to be silent and a time to speak, a time to love and a time to hate, a time for war and a time for peace.

What do workers gain from their toil? I have seen the burden God has laid on the human race. He has made everything beautiful in its time. **He has also set eternity in the human heart; yet no one can fathom what God has done from beginning to end.** *I know that there is nothing better for people than to be happy and to do good while they live. That each of them may eat and drink, and find satisfaction in all their toil—this is the gift of God. I know that everything God does will endure forever; nothing can be added to it and nothing taken from it.* **God does it so that people will fear Him.** *Whatever is has already been, and what will be has been before; and God will call the past to account. And I saw something else under the sun: In the place of judgment—wickedness was there, in the place of justice—wickedness was there. I said to myself* (King Solomon speaking here), **"God will bring into judgment both the righteous and the wicked, for there will be a time for every activity, a time to judge every deed"** (Ecclesiastes 3:1–22).

This is the Lord's testimony to those people who do not believe. I want to let them know they cannot hide away from God. Everything He said is true and remains true.

5

GOD MADE THE EARTH JUST PERFECT FOR YOU

You know, according to scientists if the sun were any nearer, we would get scorched; any further and we would get frozen. If the atmosphere contained more oxygen we wouldn't be able to breathe, and with less oxygen present we would be gasping for air. Even the distance of our planet to the sun and the moon and the stars is exactly right for life on earth. The moon regulates the coming in and going out of the sea. And as the sea comes in it brings forth new life and things get replenished. And when God causes rain to water the earth and the sun to give its heat to the plants and trees, it produces food for all the inhabitants of the earth. The food we eat, the air we breathe and everything that we need come directly from how God intended the earth to operate and to work in conjunction with what we need to survive on earth. Did you know, without the sun photosynthesis in plants would not exist? Without the rain all crops would fail; nothing can grow without sun and rain. The animals wouldn't have food (plants) to eat, and we wouldn't have food either. The truth is, everything revolves around the hand of God.

Some people may think there's no Creator. But with no one to run heaven and earth, along with the activities in the galaxy and the whole universe, planets would be colliding with each other, and I believe earth would be dysfunctional and no one could live on it. **Even a small machine needs an operator; how much more the whole universe!**

We are so unique that no two faces are identical. I could never understand people when they think things evolve and become human. **The truth is, God is the long-suffering Creator who is very patient with us all on earth.** Even the very you was created by Him. Your spirit is given to you so that you have life. He put you in your mother's womb, and then you became a living being. God gave you ability, wisdom and knowledge to understand things.

Most scientists disregard the fact that the Lord created things, and instead try to explain away Creation using the theory of evolution, saying that everything just came from a 'big bang'! What nonsense! We all know every explosion destroys everything around it—it will never ever cause anything to fuse together no matter how many observations you do with it. How could any scientist conclude that it fuses life to evolve a new life? It doesn't matter over how many years they conclude it happens, even if they say it happened trillions of years ago, it just goes against all the laws of nature and science.

And they call themselves highly intelligent individuals and they don't acknowledge that God, **the Almighty Creator—who gave them the intelligence they possess**—is behind all the things they observe and learn. Oh, they think they know this and they know that—those scientists who try to make a name for themselves; and they think every individual will just believe and agree with the theory of evolution. But it is just a theory, it is not reality and they have failed to explain everything. So they think if they let people believe that some of the events happened millions and billions of years ago their theory will silence all those inquisitive minds and disregard God's Creation! God knew all these things, that all these critics were going to try to invalidate God's truth; but their limited wisdom and intelligence came from God also!

But not all scientists disagree with God's Creation—some of them are actually beginning to believe that there is a Creator!

If we could only think soberly about how complex parts of the human body are, we would be amazed at how the brain works. There are actually parts of our brain that are connected to speech, and even emotion. Our eyes are such small parts in our head, but they can see hundreds and even maybe thousands of miles away. Here in our lovely planet we are about seven and a half billion and yet no two faces are completely identical, even among twins, triplets, quadruplets or quintets—children born of the same parents but having their own individual genetic identities. Isn't that just extraordinary information to know?

I believe some people might accept the scientists' theories because it earns them a living; and the government supports the theories of these scientists and presents it as reality. Because they say it happened billions of years ago, people's minds stop processing any more contradictions against evolution. But not when you know the Creator....

You might feel inadequate to argue against their theories because no one will believe you—you're not a scientist, you are only an ordinary person who believes in God. But I'd rather believe the heritage and the legacy of the ancient book, the Holy Bible, than to listen to scientists' imaginations concerning evolution versus Creation.

God is a Supernatural God—not subject to any human minds. A few words from God and the world was created! If God Himself did not breathe into Adam's nostrils there would be no life in him, so how could one truly believe that the molecules after the 'big bang' fused together and created life? If there really was a big bang—and it might have been **when the Lord God spoke**—it shook the heaven and also the earth (as it says in Psalm 29:8, *the voice of the Lord shakes the wilderness*). There's no life that is existing today apart from the life that God has intended to exist.

I suppose **we are all aware that our lives are borrowed and the final destination of every living being is death, physical death.** Even when scientists die, would their dead organs ever fuse together again to exist? Surely not. God gave scientists life and spirits too—that's why they are alive, just like us; **their lives are borrowed from the Creator.**

Just think about the earth's natural resources such as coal, gas, oil, and precious stones. All these things didn't just appear out of nowhere, God must have placed these natural substances underground for people to mine. Think also of the sand on the seashore, when the Lord said He put boundaries for the sea. He said, *"This far you may come and no farther; here is where your proud waves halt."* (See Job 38:8–11.) If you would just stop and think about who is responsible for all these things—even the calamities that are happening, yes even the calamities—it's God's heavens and earth. Who will tell Him or command Him to stop, or don't do this and don't do that?

Even the stars and the moon and the sea are all connected to the natural rotation of God's created world, and the surroundings we are in; it works just the way the Lord told us. Even the climates in the countries around the world are all different from each other and they are suited to certain types of plants and crops. For example: rice, bananas, guava, soya, coconuts, jackfruit, etc. only grow in tropical countries, but away from the Equator these plants will not survive. Likewise, fruits such as apples, grapes plums and pears can only be grown outside the tropics. Let me tell you, God controls the seasons of the whole wide world from heaven above to earth beneath. Try asking a scientist how that happens.

The increase of knowledge in the whole world, which was predicted in the Bible long before it happened, we can see and are experiencing right now. We are in this stage where knowledge is exploding everywhere—not just the natural knowledge as we call it, but also the spiritual knowledge in the Christian world. Spiritual knowledge is increasing and available for all believers to use; God said so!

I also found out (talking to my husband) that glass comes from grains of sand—silica sand, or the ordinary sand from the beach, that has been super-heated to very high temperatures. Sometimes when lightning strikes sand on the beach it can create a small piece of colourful glass. Some of the dye we use to colour our clothes comes from plants, but others come from sea molluscs. How magnificent is that? You might say, "Naylee, that's not new," but think about how it was first discovered by people centuries ago. We truly have an almighty, all powerful Creator that is God! Yes, think also about when rainbows appear in the sky, as it is stated in Genesis 9:12–17.

The rainbow is God's covenant between Himself, Noah, and all living creatures here on earth. God said to Noah and his children: *"This is the sign of the covenant which I make between Me and you, and every living creature that is with you, for perpetual generations:* **I set My rainbow in the cloud, and it shall be for the sign of the covenant between Me and the earth.** *It shall be, when I bring a cloud over the earth, that the rainbow shall be seen in the cloud; and I will remember My covenant which is between Me and you and every living creature of all flesh; the waters shall never again become a flood to destroy all flesh. The rainbow shall be in the cloud, and I will look on it to remember the everlasting covenant between God and every living creature of all flesh that is on the earth."* And God said to

Noah, *"This is the sign of the covenant which I have established between Me and all flesh that is on the earth."*

The time will come when the Lord will do what He has pronounced to do on earth, and this earth will be destroyed by a fervent heat. What would you say, "Stop the earth; I want to get off"? In 2 Peter 3:10–13 it says: *But the day of the Lord will come as a thief in the night, in which the heavens will pass away with a great noise, and the elements will melt with fervent heat; both the earth and the works that are in it will be burned up. Therefore, since all these things will be dissolved, what manner of persons ought you to be in holy conduct and godliness, looking for and hastening the coming of the day of God, because of which the heavens will be dissolved, being on fire, and the elements will melt with fervent heat? Nevertheless we, according to His promise, look for new heavens and a new earth in which righteousness dwells.*

If we just think about this: **all the planets are suspended between heaven and earth, and they don't just drop—so who holds them up**? And when the morning stars appear on earth these sing to the Lord, see Job 38:7. A certain scientist who believes in God's Creation declared that the galaxy makes musical sounds, peaceful and uplifting as if praising God. How much more proof from God do people want? And how could they contend with God's creation? Some so-called intellectual scientists would dare and try to prove God wrong as the Creator and God of His Creations. We didn't come from a monkey, no matter how much you compare yourself to one, as some scientists would claim. **You were created in the image and the likeness of the living God; you were made by Him and so affectionately and intimately loved and desired by Him**. Your existence was planned by Him, therefore He has a claim for your heart, soul and spirit.

I bet you, no scientist could explain where the mines of gold, silver, bronze and precious stones come from? Who formed it in the ground? And other substances like cement, lime, clay, grass; and all the animals of different species—how could any scientist explain where they came from? Charles Darwin tried to explain it away with his theory of evolution, but I know God provided all these things for us all to enjoy and to use.

GOD MADE THE EARTH JUST PERFECT FOR YOU

God commanded Moses, and other people before our time, to write this truth for us, so that we have knowledge of the past and we have knowledge of our environment. God is the Creator of all things above and under heaven.

But there will be an end to all the good things we know and see, what we are used to; everything around us will vanish and it's all written in the Bible from Genesis to Revelation. The Lord Jesus communicated these events that will happen at the end of the age, when judgement is coming to all inhabitants of the earth. It will be judgement and not love. Love when the Lord Jesus came down and ascended to heaven the first time, but judgement when He comes back the second time—for He has given all people on planet earth time to repent, and to accept His instruction through His disciples and other generations.

Every single person living now on earth will be judged, whether you believe you're good or you know you are bad, and we don't know when that day will come. Only the Father God knows the moment of Lord Jesus' return, when Father God sends Him back for the second time on earth to judge us all. So everyone needs to be ready before that time comes. See Matthew 24:36. We will go spiritually to eternal life, where God will always be God, but for those who did not believe the Son of God, to eternal condemnation. As it says in John 3:16 & 18: *For God so loved the world that He gave His only begotten Son, that* **whoever believes in Him should not perish but have everlasting life** *... but he who does not believe is* **condemned already**, *because he has not believed in the name of the only begotten Son of God.* This is the testimony of the Lord Jesus about Himself, and whether you accept it or not, **only the Testimony of the Lord Jesus, in God's Word, is valid.** And when you do accept His word you will have a close walk with God.

If you have never heard about Jesus Christ of Nazareth, perhaps you have heard of Christmas and Easter, or Holy Week. These are all part of the Jews' witnessing to the whole world—for Salvation belongs and started with the Jews. Jesus Himself was born a Jew and the Son of God at the same time.

Hey, be wise and drop the pride, because no one is exempted!

6

HE SUPPLIES ALL YOUR NEEDS

And my God shall supply all your need according to His riches in glory by Christ Jesus (Philippians 4:19). The Bible says our needs will be met by God, and He does. All good parents always supply, and sometimes go beyond, all the needs and wants of their children. In my country, the Philippines, people go abroad to work to supply all the needs of their family, especially their children, or even other members of the family. Some people work day and night to earn money for their family. And you see, God always blesses the people who use their own ability. We have a saying in my country, '**God's mercy lies for those who do works**'. We need to do the work for Him to bless us. But it also says in Deuteronomy 8:18: *But remember the Lord your God, for it is he who gives you the ability to produce wealth.* So you see everything was given to you by God.

In Matthew 6:25-34 it says: *"Therefore I say to you, do not worry about your life, what you will eat or what you will drink; nor about your body, what you will put on. Is not life more than food and the body more than clothing? Look at the birds of the air, for they neither sow nor reap nor gather into barns; yet your heavenly Father feeds them. Are you not of more value than they? Which of you by worrying can add one cubit to his stature? "So why do you worry about clothing? Consider the lilies of the field, how they grow: they neither toil nor spin; and yet I say to you that even Solomon in all his glory was not arrayed like one of these. Now if God so clothes the grass of the field, which today is, and tomorrow is thrown into the oven, will He not much more clothe you, O you of little faith?*

"For your heavenly Father knows that you need all these things. But seek first the kingdom of God and His righteousness, and all these things shall be added to you. Therefore do not worry about tomorrow, for tomorrow will worry about its own things. Sufficient for the day is its own trouble."

Even before the first human beings were created by God, the

Lord provided them with their natural needs, when He created all the fruit trees, the plants, the fish of the sea and the birds of the air—although in the beginning the Lord gave only green plants for Adam and Eve to eat. For this is what the Lord did for them: He blessed them and said, *"Let them* (Adam and Eve) *have dominion over the fish of the sea, over the birds of the air, and over the cattle, over all the earth and over every creeping thing that creeps on the earth."* The Lord God gave them green plants to eat (see Genesis 2:9) but after they sinned they could eat everything they had dominion over (see Genesis 9:3).

Also, after they sinned and obeyed the deceiver and were embarrassed to face each other and their Maker, God Himself clothed them out of the skin of an animal. This I believe was the first animal sacrifice through the shedding of blood. You cannot really take the skin of an animal without killing it, to use for someone's clothing. I believe God actually killed an animal to give Adam and Eve something to wear. Okay, maybe God could have undressed sheep instead for their clothing, but since they had sinned against God by disobeying His command they needed a remission for their sins. It says in Hebrews 9:22: *In fact, the law requires that nearly everything be cleansed with blood, and* **without the shedding of blood there is no forgiveness.**

You know, you didn't have a choice into which race you were born. God took that opportunity and decided for us. So when you think you are better than any of the people around you of a different race, like Jews, Africans or Asians etc., you are mistaken. According to the Word of God we were created equal, and it's true. All of us eat, go to the smallest room in the house, do our normal business there—believe me, that's the only throne I have got—we wash, clothe ourselves and so on.

And thank you Lord, He gave us all the ability to produce wealth and make a living, so we could have everything we need. In everything the Lord has done he thought about us: before He created a man He created plants and herbs, fruit trees, livestock, birds of the air, the crabs, the fish, and light for us to carry out our work and darkness for us to rest. God prepared everything before He made us. So we can give thanks to God He didn't place you in a foreign land with a people of obscure language that your soul could not stand. (This is just a bit of a joke.) You didn't choose your parents or siblings either, that's why we've heard a lot of people say, "You can choose your friends but you cannot choose your relatives," right? That's very true! Some people would probably think they wish they were born into royalty, because there would be such an opportunity for them to be at the centre of the world's attention.

You could probably even indulge in your thinking and show other people what you can naturally do that others cannot. It's people's nature to show off, and I think especially so when we are naturally talented. We tend to compare ourselves to those people we think are not as good as we are. We might say: "I've got a far more melodious voice," or, "I can hit the high notes far better than she does." "My family is richer than yours." "I have more achievements at my young age than she or he has." "I am stronger than her or him and more beautiful than those in the Smith family I met in Mallorca." Or maybe your parents brought you up thinking that the sun truly does shine where it doesn't. Well, whatever you have, and had, and are going to have or achieve in life, it all started with God—when He gave you that certain ability that you might have since cultivated or learned in life. The truth is we were all created equal. Can you just imagine if all people were fashion models (oh, I want to have a bit of those good looks) and fashion designers? To whom would they show off their new designs and modelling if everyone were all the same? Thank You, Lord, that You have created us all different!

Hierarchy and power are sought by everyone. When you go to a singles club, even for Christians (so I heard a few years back), some individuals think they are better than others. We are supposed to be created equal but some would say, "Hey, I'm a doctor; what is he, a cleaner?" "I'm a psychologist; what is she, a hairdresser?" Imagine a world without hairdressers; you would be walking along the high street like a bushy tree or a scarecrow—I don't think it would be a pretty sight. If there were no bakers, cooks, carpenters, engineers, dentists, janitors, street sweepers etc., we would be living in a completely dysfunctional world.

All people's professions are just jobs that they have trained to do. They have just learned to do their vocation; it is not amazingly extraordinary, as God gave us the ability in the first place! So many people stop going to these so called 'Christian clubs' because they feel their job is inferior to others. I do not know the actual statistics but a few people I know have stopped going. We are supposed to treat every individual as we would like ourselves to be treated. This florist looked down at a hairdresser and thought to herself, "I'm better than you." (What, sticking flowers in a pot? Maybe.) Non-Christians do it, so what makes you different from them? How could you claim in front of God you're a Christian when hypocrisy is reigning heavily in your heart?

Whose spirit are you following? I can assure you it's not The Holy Spirit of the living God! Okay, you may be holding a higher job position, so what? All in all we're all the same. We eat, sleep, wash and go to the smallest room in the house and so on. You might have lots of money and possessions but they won't help you avoid bad health, turmoil, or problems. We all have one destiny and you cannot take your possessions with you when you die, even if you try to strap them onto your back. They will be no use to you. Maybe even your achievements and name will soon be forgotten.

In Isaiah 3:10 it says: *Tell the righteous it will be well with them, for they will enjoy the fruits of their deeds*. And in Ecclesiastes 2:24 & 26: *A man can do nothing better than to eat and drink and find satisfaction in his work. To the man who pleases Him, God gives wisdom, knowledge and happiness, but to the sinner He gives the task of gathering and storing up wealth to hand it over to the one who pleases God.*

As Christians, we should be sober and not intoxicated with our self-image, possessions or profession. **For whoever exalts himself shall be humbled, and whoever humbles himself** (before God and men), **shall be exalted** (Matthew 23:12). And in 1 Peter 5:6: *Humble yourselves, therefore, under God's mighty hand* (a command), *that he may lift you up in due time*.

I can do all things through Christ who strengthens me.

7

JESUS SAID, "YOU MUST BE BORN AGAIN"

There is no greater instruction in the world than what the Lord Jesus said in John 3:1–15: *Now there was a Pharisee, a man named Nicodemus who was a member of the Jewish ruling council. He came to Jesus at night and said, "Rabbi, we know that you are a teacher who has come from God. For no one could perform the signs you are doing if God were not with Him."*

Jesus replied, "Very truly I tell you, no one can see the kingdom of God unless they are born again." (So this term born again came from the Lord Jesus.)

"How can someone be born when they are old?" Nicodemus asked. "Surely they cannot enter a second time into their mother's womb to be born!"

Jesus answered, "Very truly I tell you, no one can enter the kingdom of God unless they are **born of water and the Spirit***.* (Being born of water is explained in 1 Peter 3:21: *and this* **water** *symbolizes* **baptism** *that now saves you also—not the removal of dirt from the body but the pledge of a clear conscience toward God. It saves you by the resurrection of Jesus Christ.* See also Matthew 21:25; it also says that water baptism comes from heaven and not from man.) *Flesh gives birth to flesh, but the Spirit gives birth to spirit. You should not be surprised at My saying, 'You must be born again.* (**It's a command from the Lord Jesus**! Not a suggestion or statement.) *The wind blows wherever it pleases. You hear its sound, but you cannot tell where it comes from or where it is going. So it is with everyone born of the Spirit."*

"How can this be?" Nicodemus asked.

"You are Israel's teacher," said Jesus, "and do you not understand these things? Very truly I tell you, we speak of what we know, and we testify to what we have seen, but still you people do not accept our testimony. I have spoken to you of earthly things and you do not believe; how then will you believe

if I speak of heavenly things? **No one has ever gone into heaven except the one who came from heaven**—*the Son of Man. Just as Moses lifted up the snake in the wilderness, so the Son of Man must be lifted up, that everyone who believes may have eternal life in him."*

Being born again is birth in your spirit man. We were born in the flesh—that's the birth we all know, but the birthing in the spirit is to discover why you were born on earth and for what reason or purpose. Beginning in the birthing in spirit is just a word from your mouth and believing in your heart, but also belief in the Lord Jesus taking your sins upon His body on the Cross of Calvary. You might say, "How do I know that He took my sins away?" He said it this way in John 10:10: *"The thief does not come except to steal, and to kill, and to destroy.* **"I have come that they** (the world—we) **may have life,** *and that they may have it more abundantly."*

There's a thief who steals life and that is the devil. He entices people to use drugs and other bad substances or habits to have their focus on themselves. I know there are people who are more logical in their thinking and there's nothing wrong with that—the Lord Himself gave us this mind to think—but the mind-set we are operating on shouldn't only be natural; we also need the mind of Christ. That is why the Bible talks about renewing your mind, because your mind is acquainted with all the natural things we see and do. In Romans 12:2 it says: *And do not be conformed to this world, but be transformed by the renewing of your mind, that you may prove what is that good and acceptable and perfect will of God.*

Why is it so important that our minds be renewed? Believe it or not the mind is the stronghold in life. **No one can change your mind** by their will. **It has to be by your own will**, and we have our predominant will in all of us. The mind that is adherent to God's will, is the mind that could comply with God's commands. If in your humble state of mind you can seek God to help you, because He is the best help anyone can ask of, then there is hope for you. It says in Romans 8:7: *The mind governed by the flesh is hostile to God; it does not submit to God's law, nor can it do so*. It's only by a person's will that God would make Himself known. Our part is we need to submit our freewill to God; this should be our choice, for God will not impose Himself upon you, but will gently lead you by His Word, and He will use people to make His good will known to you. You may ask, "How do you know God has a good will for me?" Because God is good, that is His nature, and He never has a bad will for anyone. And there are a few that recognise and accept God's will in their lives. But there are plenty more people who just want to argue and think to themselves that those people who believe in God are weak minded and brainwashed. I'd rather have my brain washed by the word of God—because there's power and wisdom and life in God's Word—than be washed with the use of a substance that makes you not able to be yourself; like drugs, alcohol and other substances that make you feel unwell.

Most people think everything that's happening in their everyday life is irrelevant to God, who is in control of everything. And they always have that question: "If God is so powerful, why this and that and what about all the bad things that are happening?" But God said, "Call unto Me." The majority of people's thoughts are far from God, and they do not call on Him, even in their distresses. Perhaps it never entered into their minds to call on Him, so they swear instead.

We see how evil the world is now—whenever we hear news it's all bad news. All that sexual immorality that's happening right now, all the killing of innocent people, and the human trafficking, where they trap and subject those unfortunate people to fear and tell them they owe such an amount for staying in the hotel, and the food they eat. But these buyers and sellers of people know their evil deeds. How could you sell people you don't own, except by fooling them to get a job that does not exist, with, sometimes, people they trusted? For the sake of good, I hope their conscience will be seared with compassion for those poor victims of crime, crime that they're gaining material wealth from, which is utterly diabolical.

Before the dreadful day of the Lord comes—when He will judge all inhabitants of the heaven and earth, and even under the earth, and dominions and kingdoms visible and invisible—before that day comes, please repent and call on the Name of the Lord Jesus and you will be saved, saved from the worst-ever disaster the world is going to have to face.

JESUS SAID, "YOU MUST BE BORN AGAIN"

You see, it says in Leviticus 18:28: ... *lest the land vomit you out also when you defile it, as it vomited out the nations that were before you.* The earth has vomited out its people in the past because of all the ungodly works they did, so how much more now that you hear extremity of bad events happening. We really badly need God's protection for our lives. This is a warning to all and it says in Matthew 10:28: **"And do not fear those who kill the body but cannot kill the soul. But rather fear Him who is able to destroy both soul and body in hell."** (This was the Lord Jesus teaching His disciples whom to fear. Not to fear humans but to fear God, who is higher than humans; no comparison, humans are created by God!)

Also in Ezekiel 33:11: *Say to them: 'As I live,' says the Lord God, 'I have no pleasure in the death of the wicked, but that the wicked turn from his way and live. Turn, turn from your evil ways! For why should you die O house of Israel?'* Although God was referring to the house of Israel in those days, today all people living are included; since **the Lord Jesus died for the whole world, not just for the Israelites**, and gave His life for us all, now no one is exempted.

My question is, "Do you know where your spirit is going to after you die physically?" And as much as we try to prepare our going out of this world, when we know we have only to rot in the soil our feet are walking on, we too need to know where our spirit man will really stay after it leaves our physical bodies. I know you might well say, "You told us it will return to the One it came from," but the situation is out of your hand once you die; that's why the Lord Jesus is giving us a chance to choose Him, and to be with Him. The Lord said, *"Abide in Me, and I in you,"* see John 15:4–6, and it also says in 1 John 2:6: *Whoever claims to abide in Him must walk as Jesus walked.* The Lord said, "*He who believes in Him is not condemned; but he who does not believe is condemned already, because he has not believed in the name of the only begotten Son of God*" (John 3:18). And He is the witness and He is not just witnessing for Himself; a lot of old prophets and His disciples, including John the Baptist, witnessed about Him being the Messiah, the One sent by God; the baptiser of the Holy Spirit, the miracle Maker, the Mighty One of God. And God gave us a choice because of His love for us all; He gave us a choice, because he loved everything He created and He said, "*It is good.*"

The Angels who sinned intentionally will be judged too. For they knew right from wrong from the start, otherwise they wouldn't be called Angels. It says in 2 Peter 2:4–6: *For **if God did not spare angels when they sinned, but sent them to hell, putting them in chains of darkness to be held for judgement;** if He did not spare the ancient world when He brought the flood on its ungodly people, but protected Noah, a preacher of righteousness, and seven others; **if He condemned the cities of Sodom and Gomorrah by burning them to ashes, and made them an example of what is going to happen to the ungodly*....

If God did not spare the Angels who sinned, what do you think? Could you be spared? Wake up and don't be stubborn! And we know right from wrong, and we still have a choice to seek God, to believe Him or to ignore His warning. I try to obey so as not to lose my place in God's kingdom. We will all be there one day if we believe Jesus' Word, so this is where His invitation begins.

I want to ask you, "**Do you fear dying?**" If you do, here are some of the facts you need to know. I believe you will only be afraid of dying if you do not know where your spirit is going when you die. You might say, "I'm too young to think of that and I am not going to die yet." The reality is life is too short; an illness or an accident might send you earlier than you expected. I am not writing this to frighten you, not at all, I just want to make you aware that God is for you. When you know Him, you're assured you'll be with Him, when your spirit leaves your body.

I heard that some Christians are afraid of dying. I believe this is because they have no assurance from the Holy Spirit that their relationship with God is for real.

Let me just say this first, that fear is the opposite of faith, faith in God, okay. True faith comes from within, in your spirit man from your heart. You might say, "How could I put my faith in God whom I do not see or do not experience?" **Let me just remind you of your personal experience, when you were a little child.** Did you ever see something that grown-up people never saw? Only you saw it, and you didn't even talk to anyone about it when you were little, at that age? Or if you did, the person you talked to didn't see it? You probably weren't scared when you saw it, but you were surprised to have seen it, and you still remember it now that you are older; yes? What has this got to do with fear versus faith? What I mean is, you experience something out of the ordinary; it exists—right? But is it just in your own experience—yes? And you might not be aware of it, but out of the ordinary you experienced something spiritual. God is Spirit. When you experience faith in God, it doesn't make you fearful, because you've got the assurance of His love.

You might be fearful of dying because you do not know God and His love for you, and you may be thinking that God doesn't know you. The truth is, God called your spirit, put you in your mother's womb and gave life to you. The conception through your mum and dad's participation is the physical putting into action of what God intended you to be. Just like the Lord Jesus; He was that Word that God spoke in Creation. That was His name in heaven before creation—the WORD, when He was with the Father God and the Holy Spirit, ok? (The Spirit was hovering over the surface of the deep, yes?) But before He came down on earth, even the Prophet Isaiah, King David, and the other prophets talked about His coming on earth. And the reason is to make our spirit man alive in Him, whom Adam and Eve, maybe almost from the beginning of time, accidentally put to sleep. If you're thinking now, "What have Adam and Eve got to do with me?" well, through so many generations they were your forefathers, and no human being was born without them.

We don't know how long they lived in the Garden of Eden before they sinned and became subject to the devil. When the Lord God said to Adam, *"you shall surely die"* (see Genesis 2:17), **that word 'die' means physically dying and decaying, but never finishing dying.** It is the process of continuously decaying and dying, but not coming to an end. That sounds like hell to me. And the Lord said He had no pleasure in the wicked going to hell. That's why the Lord Jesus came, and the Lord Jesus could not have come if Adam or Eve had touched the tree of life. The tree of knowledge of good and evil was the testing object for people to obey God wholeheartedly, forever. But the Lord knew they would not always obey God forever, for He said, **When** *you eat of it, you shall surely die* (see Genesis 2:17).

Continuously dying is the fearful thing a person could face when their spirit leaves their body, and the only thing that will save all of us is to believe in the Lord Jesus, that He is the only way, the truth and the life and that He died for you and me, to take your sin and mine away. No man comes to the Father (He is our God) except through Him (the Lord Jesus).

Father God prepared everything from the ancestral line of Seth, the third son of Adam, who had a son named Enoch and was taken by God. He was known as the man who pleased God in his time and didn't taste death. It says in Hebrews 11:6: *But without faith it is impossible to please Him: for he who comes to God must believe that He is, and that He is the rewarder of those who diligently seek Him.* God included Him in the lineage of Adam to Joseph (Jacob's son), from Joseph to King David, from King David to the Lord Jesus. The only way we can please God is when we have faith in Him; when we believe and obey and walk rightly before Him. God took Enoch alive—he didn't experience natural death—because he walked with God.

God chose Abram and called him Abraham—meaning 'father of many'—and Sarai, whom God named Sarah—'princess'. In their old age they had a son whom God had promised for them to have, because Sarah was barren. So Isaac was born and then fathered Jacob, but God changed Jacob's name to Israel (the present country itself). God chose Israel for Himself for His people to dwell in. King David, who descended from Jacob, sinned but God still considered him as a man after His own heart, see Acts 13:22.

After Adam and Eve sinned we were all born sinners, born of flesh, of a man's will. But **the Lord Jesus was born by the will of God**, and worked and lived in obedience to God, **and died in the will of God**. The Lord Jesus said: *"I am the way, the truth, and the life. No one comes to the Father except through Me"*(John 14:6). And in John 1:3–4 it says: *In Him* (the Lord Jesus) *was life, and the life was the light of men.* So **without the Lord Jesus there would be no light, and no life on earth.** *All things were made through Him,* (the Lord Jesus) *and without Him nothing was made that was made.*

And to back it up with another scripture it says in Colossians 1:15–18: *He is **the image of the invisible God**, the firstborn over* *all creation. For by Him all things were created that are in heaven and that are on earth, visible and invisible, whether thrones or dominions or principalities or powers. All things were created through Him and for Him. And He is before all things, and in Him all things consist. And He is the head of the body, the church, who is the beginning, the firstborn from the dead, that in all things He may have the pre-eminence.* And In Colossians 1:12–14: *giving thanks to the* **Father who has qualified us** *to be partakers of the inheritance of the saints in the light. He has delivered us from the power of darkness and conveyed us into the kingdom of the Son of His love, in whom* **we have redemption through His blood, the forgiveness of sins.**

There is one condition: you have to believe the Lord Jesus died for you and that you are a sinner and need a Saviour, so that He may forgive and redeem you. In fact, what He did no one can undo; He has already redeemed you but you need only to accept Him and accept that He totally sacrificed His life for you, that you may have life in Him. This is our faith in the Christ of God, who gave us a window to the future so we can continue to live a life without fear of dying.

If in your mind you cannot really reach that thought of the Lord Jesus dying for you, then ask Him. Say "Lord Jesus, if this is true, please show me your face, and help me to believe in You." He said, *"Ask, and it will be given to you; seek, and you will find; knock, and it will be opened to you. For everyone who asks receives, and he who seeks finds, and to him who knocks it will be opened"* (Matthew 7:7–8).

You may think the Lord doesn't know you. You are mistaken; God knows everyone. He dedicated His entire life to know you through the Lord Jesus. Do you want to hear Him call your name? Ask and listen, He will never fail you ... So God knows your name and even your personality, and your heart.

In my first book, titled, 'Can you really hear from God Nowadays', I said I believed the Lord enabled me to recognise Elijah, the prophet of God, in my dreams—whom I had never met on earth, of course. (How could I?) And the power of his pointing at me made me bow down to him, as if some power or force pushed me down helpless with my face to the ground. He heard my whisper although I was so far away from him. You know, **it's the spirit of a man that recognises a man**. I saw Elijah's form—he looked very slim, and had weathered skin; quite an old man with whitish hair and a beard. He was not very tall but well respected. You see, we were spirit before we were born; how could the Lord call us otherwise, when our physical ears weren't yet formed? So He knows you, and has power over you.

I think there's no point in disregarding the fact that God is God over the heavens and the earth, since God created the earth and all that is in it, see Psalms 24:1–2: *The earth is the Lord's and everything in it, the world, and all who live in it; for He founded it upon the seas and established it upon the waters.*

And because you are at present living on one of His planets, Earth, that He created so beautifully with the animals and everything else—the flowers, the fruit trees for our daily needs, the hills and seas, and valleys and plains and all of the things we taste and touch and smell and see—isn't that amazing enough just to know that the Creator is also our loving God, and the Father of our spirit man?

He has in fact allowed you to stay and enjoy everything you have right now and has freely given you the right to live on planet Earth. He wants all the best for you, and most of all He wants you to know Him; that is your part to play. You must acknowledge God as the provider of your daily needs. Have you realised how important God's daily provision is for the earth?

When you feel overwhelmed with the problems you are facing and you need help, you know God will help you when you ask Him. He is a gentle God and He would never intrude in your life or overtake you. If you have a personal relationship with the Lord Jesus and you agree to let Him lead you and guide you always, then He could show you the way you should go. He knows when you sit and when you rise, He knows your thoughts afar off. He knows your coming and going; He said He knows you all together (see Psalm 139:2–4). And all His thoughts towards you are holy, full of love and compassion to keep you safe and not be afraid of anything. If you don't have a relationship with the Son of God, you don't have that protection, but **if you have a relationship with God, you need not be afraid of dying**.

JESUS SAID, "YOU MUST BE BORN AGAIN"

In Isaiah 53:7 it says: *He (Jesus) was oppressed and He was afflicted, yet He opened not His mouth; He was led as a lamb to the slaughter, and as a sheep before its shearers is silent, so He did not open His mouth.* See, the Lord Jesus did not challenge His opponents (teachers of the law, the Pharisees and some Jews) and charge anyone with wrong doing.

So if someone asks you how a loving and all powerful God could allow bad things to happen to innocent people, and why He didn't stop it, if He is that powerful, let me also ask you a question: How could a loving Father God, who is all powerful, omnipotent, omniscient and omnipresent, allow His Son—His only begotten Son whom He is well pleased with—**to die on the Cross for you and me**?

In the Lord Jesus' human will, He didn't want to die, but He knew why He had come down to earth to live as a human in the flesh. It was to do the will of His Father, our God, which no human could do; He alone could do it. The Lord Jesus was not selfish in His Godly being, He humbly let His Father, our God, take over in His situation; He didn't call a battalion of Angels to rescue Him from the hands of His perpetrators. He knew that no Angel and no other human being could ever take His place in the assignment that Father God had called Him to.

When our Lord was born as a human, He too had freewill (see Matthew 26:53), but for His sacrifice to complete the work of God, He humbly submitted Himself to the Father God's will, and not to His human will or freedom. Remember, when He was on earth He was half-God and half-human, and in His human will He prayed to His Father that he might be spared death. See Matthew 26:39–44: *He went a little farther and fell on His face, and prayed, saying, "O My Father, if it is possible, let this cup pass from Me; nevertheless, **not as I will, but as You will**."*

Can you still further imagine, when the Lord Jesus was on the Cross, He prayed to His Father, our God, saying, *"Forgive them, Father, for they know not what they are doing"*? The Lord knew that He would be betrayed and denied by His own disciples, men who were with Him and taught by Him every day. He knew all these things before they happened! The Lord Jesus didn't throw a tantrum at them and didn't have a pity party for Himself. He faced it all and said to those present with Him, ***"For this*** *purpose, I was born."* He said, *"Love covers a multitude of sins."* He didn't expose them, He covered them.

Let me tell you, if God stopped or killed all bad people doing bad things—every single person who does wrong—the earth would be empty—uninhabited! *For all have sinned and fall short of the glory of God* (Romans 3:23). It also says in Ecclesiastes 7:14: *There is NOT a righteous man on earth who does what is right and never sins.* A Fact!

And we are now under construction with our characters while we are here on earth so the new heaven and earth that is coming down from heaven will be the same as the first one God had made. And on that new heaven and earth there wouldn't be a single memory of our present heaven and earth:

In Revelation 21:1-8: Then I saw *"a new heaven and a new earth," for the first heaven and the first earth had passed away, and there was no longer any sea. I saw the Holy City, the new Jerusalem, coming down out of heaven from God, prepared as a bride beautifully dressed for her husband. And I heard a loud voice from the throne saying, "Look! God's dwelling place is now among the people, and he will dwell with them. They will be His people, and God Himself will be with them and be their God. 'He will wipe every tear from their eyes. There will be no more death' or mourning or crying or pain,* **for the old order of things has passed away."**

He who was seated on the throne said, "I am making everything new!" Then he said, **"Write this down, for these words are trustworthy and true."**

He said to me (It was the Lord Jesus speaking to John His disciple in Patmos in Greece, when He was put in prison there by the Jews. John saw the Revelation of the Lord; that is what this Book of the Bible—the Testimony of the Lord Jesus to us all on earth—is about) : *"It is done. I am the Alpha and the Omega, the Beginning and the End. To the thirsty I will give water without cost from the spring of the water of life. Those who are victorious will inherit all this, and I will be their God and they will be my children. But the cowardly, the unbelieving, the vile, the murderers, the sexually immoral, those who practice magic arts, the idolaters and all liars—they will be consigned to the fiery lake of burning sulphur.* **This is the second death."**

JESUS SAID, "YOU MUST BE BORN AGAIN"

The devil doesn't have any right to touch you if Jesus is your Lord and Saviour, because you belong to Him forever. In fact it says a man that is born of the Spirit of God does not continue sinning, for the Spirit of God is in him. It's only through the power of Holy Spirit living within you, that will stop you from sinning. 1 John 3:9 says: *Whoever has been born of God does not sin, for His seed remains in him; and he cannot sin, because he has been born of God.*

But you cannot say once you're a Christian you will never sin, because humans are still subject to the lies of the devil, and we are prone to listen to him.

God promised that He will look after His people, when they call, and you cannot call Him if you don't know Him or you do not have a relationship with Him. If you acknowledge Him as your Saviour, He comes and offers you help. He expects you to come just as you are; come to Him with a sincere heart.

God knows our everyday life is hectic and we are bound with all sorts of heaviness, not just the physical heaviness (hard work) but also the heaviness in our minds and our souls, something that no human effort could erase or lighten up. The Lord Jesus knows these things, as He lived on earth for thirty-three years. He experienced all humans' emotions—heaviness of soul, heart and mind. The Lord Jesus knows every emotion you may have and He was accustomed to it all. In fact He was betrayed, and sold for thirty pieces of silver, by Judas Iscariot (see Matthew 26:15).

When the Lord Jesus was being tempted by the devil, after fasting for forty days and forty nights, the Lord replied to the adversary three times and said, "It is written". Everything about Jesus was written in the scrolls, by the old Prophets like Zechariah, Isaiah, etc. All things before they happened to the Lord Jesus here on earth were written in the Word of God. The fact that He would be sold for thirty pieces of silver is written in Zechariah 11:13, in the Old Testament—long before Jesus was born. And in Isaiah 9:6 & 7: *For to us a child is born, to us a Son is given, and the government will be on His shoulders and He will be called Wonderful Counsellor, Mighty God, Everlasting Father, Prince of Peace. Of the greatness of His government and peace there will be no end. He will reign on David's throne and over His kingdom, establishing and upholding it with justice and righteousness from that time on and for ever. The zeal of the Lord Almighty will accomplish this.*

Also in Isaiah, chapter 53:1–6 & 12: *Who has believed our message and to whom has the arm of the Lord been revealed? He grew up before Him like a tender shoot, and like a root out of dry ground. He had no beauty or majesty to attract us to Him, nothing in His appearance that we should desire Him. He was despised and rejected by mankind,* **a man of suffering, and familiar with pain.** *Like one from whom people hide their faces He was despised, and we held Him in low esteem.*

Surely He took up our pain and bore our suffering, *yet we considered Him punished by God, stricken by Him, and afflicted. But He was pierced for our transgressions, He was crushed for our iniquities; the punishment that brought us peace was on Him,* **and by His wounds we are healed.** *We all, like sheep, have gone astray, each of us has turned to our own way; and the Lord has laid on Him the iniquity of us all.*

For He (**Lord Jesus**) **bore the sin of many, and made intercession for the transgressors.**

His life and death on earth were predestined by God the Father, before He was born of Mary, His mother. Being born in the flesh is the human part of Him. He came in the flesh, see 1 John 4:2–3: *By this you know the Spirit of God: Every spirit that confesses that Jesus Christ has come in the flesh is of God, and every spirit that does not confess that Jesus Christ has come in the flesh is not of God. And this is the spirit of the Antichrist, which you have heard was coming, and is now already in the world.*

So the devil could not accuse the Lord Jesus saying: "You've never been a man, you never knew what it was like to be a man." The Lord Jesus was fully God and fully man: He wept seeing Lazarus' tomb, He was questioned and He was persecuted by the Jews, who were the law givers in His time, but He was their Master too. He washed the feet of His disciples and experienced being denied by Peter three times, who feared dying with Him at the hands of those law givers. (See John 11:35, 13:1–17, 18:15–22.)

The Lord Jesus' own brothers did not even believe Him, when He told them who He was. Although they had the same mother, if their mother told His siblings how He'd been conceived then they wouldn't have known who He really was, I suppose. If I were around then in the same family unit, I would probably be fascinated with all He did, and be amazed at the work He was doing, but would I believe Him completely to be the Son of God? I don't know; I would probably have doubted Him too. But hopefully I would have seen that all the things He did—all the miracles—were God's work, not of man, but they saw Him only as a man, not as the Son of God, which He had claimed. But obviously they attributed all these things they witnessed about Him to man, and not to the Son of God.

On His crucifixion His assailants removed His undergarment to humiliate Him. He was pushed down to utter disgrace, degraded and humiliated—not just physically but also in His soul. He was tortured mentally, emotionally, physically and spiritually; lashed by a whip that had glass embedded in the ends to actually rip His flesh open once the ends of that whip pulled away from Him. (That's where we can claim that by His wounds we are healed, see Isaiah 53:5.) But why? Because He claimed the truth that God is His Father, who sent Him to earth (who is the God of all creation), and sentenced His own Son to death, so that we (humans, the world), could be brought back near Him.

Who are we that God the Father has valued us more than His only begotten Son, that He would send Him to die for you and me, knowing how wicked and corrupt and rebellious and stubborn and sinful we are? But why are we so privileged? Because Father God looked at His Son and knew He was the only remedy; He is the only sinless, humble, gracious enough **One that holds the truth of God, and never lies**; the One who holds the life of human beings whom God the Father, Son and the Holy Spirit, created in His own image. I am ashamed that it was my sin who hung Him on that bitter Cross. And you cannot say that is just for you Naylee, and not for me, otherwise you are denying the only One who can save you from being burned in hell. Remember the rich man who was in torment in hell, and saw Lazarus being comforted, by his Father in faith, Abraham.

So do not underestimate or ignore what the Lord Jesus did for you, as an individual, and for us, as a nation. We are the fallen victims of the devil—the enemy of our souls, mind and spirit, who from the beginning became the enemy of our God and the Lord Jesus.

At the end of the day it's your soul that God cares about and values most; and the Lord Jesus does not want you to be deceived twice by the enemy of your soul. You might say, "Well, I don't believe in all of that. Well, let it be known to you right now, **Jesus was not joking when He was hung on the Cross,** and it would not change the fact that it happened (and it couldn't change His word that was written in the Bible) and that God warned us all; not just the Christians who are believers now, but also those non-Christians who do not believe yet.

If humans can study what God has done in nature and make it known to everyone, with physical and scientific evidence, **how much more should we be taught the spiritual side of life**? I can assure you that you are alive because you've got a spirit in you that will live forever and ever. But if you're just wise enough to sit back and think, then you may discover more than just what is visible.

In 2 Corinthians 12:1–5 Paul was taken up to the third heaven and saw things which he was not allowed to utter on the earth. Surely there was a secret in heaven, but we are allowed to know what has been revealed to us on earth. God who was the Creator is invisible, but I saw Him who is invisible when I prayed and asked to see Him. I saw Him in two forms; as a suffering Messiah, in a white robe, and one in a wine colour robe, healthy looking. So He *could* be visible to those He want to see Him.

And, if you think it's wise to deny God's existence, even though you know the fact of life here on earth that you will die one day (you may not know this but you wouldn't be exempted or be able to make excuses that you really did not even hear or know about God, and heaven and hell), God will require an accounting for your soul and what you did on earth. **Your life is lent to you by God**; and if you could really say to yourself without even a hint or a shadow of a doubt that you have never ever sinned against anyone or against God, then you really don't need a Saviour.

Why do we need to be born again? The Lord Jesus told a man called Nicodemus that he needed to be born again saying, *"That which is born of the flesh is flesh, and that which is born of the*

JESUS SAID, "YOU MUST BE BORN AGAIN"

spirit is spirit." If Jesus could say to you right now, "You must be born again," what do you think is the purpose of being born again? To die again after we die in the flesh? Wouldn't you think He is giving you a hint that there is truly life after death?

Our will needs to be born in the spirit, for the will and the nature of flesh is greed and self-centredness, but the nature and the will of the spirit is holiness, righteousness and peace, because our spirit comes from God. The will of the flesh is unrighteousness and rebellion towards God. So our spirit man needs to demolish the will of our soul to connect us back to God, in which we have the promise of eternal life.

As I said, the Lord Jesus didn't need to suffer for the whole world physically if we did not have any spirit worth rescuing. We know God is a just God, and He wouldn't fight with one lower than Him, because He knows there wouldn't be any point in fighting, as the battle would be won before it began. Since God is just and stands up for justice, He could only make the battle (and it is a battle) fair and just by sending the Lord Jesus as a human being.

When the Word (that's the Lord Jesus) was with God in heaven, as the governing chief of the Angels in heaven, He could not fight the fallen Angel as chief of the Angels, so honouring God and loving the creation He made, He openly and lovingly gave up His position in heaven to be human on earth. And He graciously accepted His role as a human sacrifice, because He loved what He had created.

The Lord Jesus fought the devil from this lower position as a human being, but because He was obedient to Father God's calling in His whole life as a human and as God's Son on earth, He won the battle fairly and squarely for us human beings.

By believing and obeying Father God's will for Him on earth, Jesus Christ our Lord and Saviour is our model in life.

The human side of Jesus is shown in Psalm 22:1 when He said, *"My God, My God, why have You forsaken Me?"* Also in the Gospels of Matthew and Mark and in John 12:27: *"Now My soul is troubled, and what shall I say? 'Father, save Me from this hour'? But for this purpose I came to this hour."*

He need not have died if we could just walk into heaven free of charge; but we can't, because the devil caused

judgement to come on men.

If you're not born again, the devil will always remind you and accuse you of any sins you have committed (and believe me he will always remind you, even when you're already dead). The memory of it will be present in your head and embedded in your soul, if you have not asked the Saviour to forgive you. If you ever agree with the devil that you are not a sinner, then your pride will bring you down to hell with him in a ball of fire and a great big bang. Only the Holy Spirit of God that is left here on earth to guide us and the cleansing power of the Lord Jesus' blood can clean your conscience against the accusations of the devil.

You may ask, "Why are we Christians always banging on about Jesus?" It's because we cannot help telling you all about the truth. When Jesus said, *"I am the way, the truth and the life; no man comes to the Father* (that's our God) *except through Me,"* He's telling the truth. Everything was made for Him (Jesus), and through Him, see John 1:3. Dominion and power and might are from Him. *For by Him all things were created that are in heaven and that are on earth, visible and invisible, whether thrones or dominions or principalities or powers.* ***All things were created through Him and for Him.*** *And He is before all things and in Him all things consist. And He is the head of the body the church, who is the beginning, the firstborn from the dead, that in all things He may have the pre-eminence* (Colossians 1:16–18). No one else in the planets, whether on earth or even in heaven, can claim such a statement concerning Jesus, because it's the truth.

People come and go and no-one has ever said or testified that they have died on the Cross and come back to life walking and speaking to their people for forty days, and then were taken up to heaven again, see Acts 1:9–11. Thank God no one ever has ever claimed that yet; but in the end of time the Bible says some will come and claim to be the Lord Jesus and even perform a miracle of making fire come down from heaven to deceive even the elect. But on that day only the Lord Jesus has the true answer for you.

Now in this part the Lord's Apostle John is telling us his testimony of the revelation the Lord Jesus showed while he was in Patmos, in prison for his faith in the Lord our God: *Then I, John, saw the holy city, New Jerusalem, coming down out of heaven from God, prepared as a bride adorned for her husband. And I heard a loud voice from heaven saying, "Behold, the tabernacle of God is with men, and He will dwell with them, and they shall be His people. God Himself will be with them and be their God. And God will wipe away every tear from their eyes;* **there shall be no more death**, *nor sorrow, nor crying. There shall be no more pain,* ***for the former things have passed away***" (Revelation 21: 2–4).

You may not agree with me, but you made a pact with God to be born on earth. What do I mean by this? This is what the Lord said, "Before I formed you in the womb I knew you." The fact is God gave you a freedom of choice: to be born, or not to be born in the flesh. You were a spirit before you were born; how could you hear God otherwise, when you didn't have ears yet? He is an invisible God, and our spirit is invisible.

The Lord chose your parents to whom you were to be born, and decided where you were to live on His planet earth. But the Lord Jesus said, "*You must be born again*," born of the spirit, see John 3:3–7. It's other way around for the Lord Jesus, He was already with God sinless, and became flesh still sinless, went under the law of sinners and remained sinless in God's sight, but we were born sinful, of the flesh, far away from God, and the Lord Jesus gave us the instruction to be born again of the spirit, to be brought near Him. You cannot inherit the Kingdom of God unless you are born in spirit. Being 'born again' is a command, it is not optional. It's a declaration of His truth, why He came and died, and lives again.

His invitation is simple: to be born again, and come to know Him, and be led by the Holy Spirit of the Living God.

8

THE LORD JESUS IS THE ONLY ONE WHO CAN COMPLETE YOU

Have you ever felt or thought to yourself that there is something missing in you, and you tried to fill it with all sorts of things, like a hobby, a sport or exercise, a healthy eating regime, or anything else that you feel would make you complete—even drugs, smoking, sex, etc.—but you still felt there is a massive void or hole within you that you cannot quite explain what it is? The truth is God created you that way so that you would call on Him; **the void within you is the hole that only God can fill**, so you would come to know Him who knows you and created you.

It's God's will for you to know Him, and find Him. It's like when you were little and you know it's only your mum that can make you feel better, and at peace within yourself. I'm not comparing God to your mum, that is your natural instinct. When I am in those thoughts now that I'm an adult, I call that sense or feeling *mummified*; all you need is your mum's touch and her soothing voice. It's also like wanting and needing love, care, and affection from anyone close to you, when your mum is not around, like your dad, your spouse, your siblings or even your own children.

We also have that feeling towards God when our spirit man gets awoken by God's spirit, the Holy Spirit. Our senses become aware of the things around us, which I can only explain as the Spirit-sense—higher than the natural things you and I know.

And this is not unusual; maybe a lot of us think, "Is there anything else beyond this life? What are we all doing here on earth?" Is it just: you were born, you went to school to study, then you got older, got a job, and then you got a wife, or a husband, then one day you're just gone; and all those people you cared about, you left them all sad and missing you? Well, I believe there is more to life than this, and there is life after death, when the physical stops and the spirit kicks in to re-start your life again. You may think, "What then after my spirit lives again without my body?" It says in 1 Corinthians 15:44 that all of us will have spiritual bodies, and science cannot explain this spirit side of life, because the explanation of the natural and the physical all ends with the matter of hearing, seeing, and touching. While the spirit realm is to do with knowing without seeing first, and then the experience after. It's like you know in your mind there is something that exists, like the wind; though you can't touch or see it, you feel it. Faith is like that, and faith could explain science, but science could not explain beyond the natural, like the events in the Bible. For instance, the parting of the Red Sea by Moses, so the Israelites could cross over on dry ground in the middle of the sea; Jonah swallowed by the whale and vomited onto dry ground after he prayed; Daniel in the lion's den, who wasn't harmed because he trusted His God; and how about the birth of Jesus Himself?

I can tell you of personal experiences, like for instance when this Christian lady was praying for me, and she laid her hands on my back. I got this warm sensation in my legs that was soothing and calming. Or when this person raised his hands above me and I fell on the ground. He didn't touch or push me but there was this weight or power that made me lie down on the ground; **science would not be able to explain that**!

And because of God's love for all His creation, He stepped into human shoes. Also, when God created the heavens He didn't leave them uninhabited; He put His Angels there to occupy heaven, or the heavens, and these angels were given choices just like us. And not just to know Him and obey Him, but they were also given the freedom of expression among themselves and others too. Just like them, we too have been given a choice. God didn't give us a choice to benefit Him, for the Lord could not be benefited with our choices, because all the things we have all came from Him in the first place. He had no other reason but to form a close relationship with us. He foreknew and valued us because ... HE loves us all, His Creation.

He came to earth and gladly stepped into human shoes, to redeem us humans from the inherited sins of our ancestors and from what our sinful nature dictates. **Earth could not come up to heaven, therefore heaven came down to the earth** He Created.

And because God loves us, He also commanded us to love one another as we love ourselves. It would not hurt Him physically if we don't love each other, but out of His great love for us He would feel the emotional pain of hurting human hearts. Because we are created in His image, every time He looks at us He sees Himself. The reason we are commanded to love each other is so we can enjoy life on earth. This life we have on earth is like a training ground for us, because when we reach heaven after we physically die, no one will have to command us to love one another—we will already know how to do that because we practised it here on earth.

Let me take you to what God said in Genesis 6:5–8: *The Lord saw how great man's wickedness on the earth had become, and that every inclination of the thoughts of his heart was only evil all the time. **The Lord was grieved** that He had made man on the earth, and **His heart was filled with pain**.* You can see that it says in this part that because of the wickedness of people, God's heart was in pain. People give pain to people; and God's heart, full of love for the people He created, feels the pain of those in pain. *So the Lord said, "I will wipe mankind, whom I have created, from the face of the earth—men and animals, and creatures that move along the ground, and the birds of the air—**for I Am grieved that I have made them.**"*

Maybe the animals behaved better than the people, yet because the earth became corrupt God would remove everyone. *But Noah found favour in the eyes of the Lord.* **That's why we are alive today**! We are all descended from Noah—thank God for Noah; he walked with God, our God. He is a relational God, wanting to have a relationship with us, but not forcefully. He asks us to love one another, because if we fight among each other, we will not be hurting just each other but we will be fighting against God too; and it means an act of disobedience on our side is hurtful towards God.

When you start believing God, your spirit has the power to conquer the enemy, and be under the authority of God and of the Holy Spirit. Then we are under the umbrella of the Lord Jesus' protection because we chose Him—we allowed Him to look after us and care for us. But you are not instantly under His care; you've got to tell Him you want Him and need Him to care and

THE LORD JESUS IS THE ONLY ONE WHO CAN COMPLETE YOU

to guide and to look after you, because **He will not overstep to encroach in your life, because of the freedom He gave you**. He is inviting you, **but He also needs an invitation from you to include Him in your life**, and for you to accept Him as your Lord and Saviour and protector of your life forever and ever till your spirit man returns to Him.

So I want to remind you that **the Lord Jesus' invitation is** not physical but **spiritual**. It is called, or rather we call it, **Salvation party on earth**, or **recognition party in heaven** (who God is to you and who you are in God).

When you invite Him back in your heart, the enemy cannot accuse you of wrong doing, because of the Lord Jesus' grace extended to you. You have been washed by the blood of the Lord and you are covered under the umbrella of God's protection and provision, because you accepted the Lord Jesus as your Saviour, protector and keeper of your life forevermore, so that your spirit will become alive in Him. And I can assure you, you will feel the connection with God if you take Him for real in your life.

Every human being has a spirit; the breath of life is the spirit from God. Adam became a living being after God breathed in his nostrils the breath of life. He was clay, in the form of a man, when God created him. It's the same when we see dead bodies; no spirit in them just a body—a carcass. That's why when our spirit leaves our body, we die. But believe me or not, I know the spirit of a man lives forever. Ever heard of those who have had an after- or near-death experience, when they died for a few minutes or hours then came back to life again? Most of them experience heaven, meet the Lord Jesus, and get sent back to earth to tell of the experience they had in heaven. The Lord gave some of these people the experience of seeing what hell is like too. So when we truly die we will either go to live forever with the Lord Jesus in heaven, where the recognition party is going on, or be forever dead in hell. Hell is real too, you know.

It says in Psalms 9:17: *The wicked shall be turned into hell, and all the nations that forget God.* Our spirit man needs rescuing from the clout of the devil. The earth at the moment belongs to him. If we are born-again believers in Christ Jesus of Nazareth we are sojourners with our brothers and sisters in the Lord. We are passers-by, pilgrims; this is not the home for our soul. Our home is heaven-bound where the Lord Jesus sits at the right hand of the throne of the Living God! Jesus our Lord is the only One that has the power to rescue me and you, and without our faith in Jesus, and the redeeming power of His blood through the outworking of the Holy Spirit for us, we can do nothing.

When we receive the Lord Jesus as our personal Saviour and protector, we receive His invitation to live with Him forever in heaven. Because God has given us freewill, we are indeed free to choose Him and follow His will. But if we wouldn't follow Him, we might start to follow the devil and we wouldn't know we're following him; he will not represent himself to us as a snake now but as a whispering spirit in our head, and we may even think it's our own thoughts. This devil is the spirit of the anti-Christ who deceived people like Adam and Eve. As we know, they died spiritually, as if they were in a spiritual coma.

And if Adam or Eve had touched the tree of life they, and we, would be forever sinful, with no remedy for all human creation. The Lord Jesus could not come down to earth and humans would be spiritually doomed, and forever sinful for the rest of eternity—no Saviour could save us. Jesus' life on earth was to submit to Father God and sacrifice His own freewill to Father God, for all us humans to be saved from the hands of the devil that Adam and Eve had ignorantly obeyed. Why did I say ignorantly? Because at that time they didn't know how to sin—they didn't know what was right and how to act wrong; all they knew was not to touch and not to eat from the tree of the knowledge of good and evil—that's all they knew. But they were both deceived by the devil, big time.

But what the devil meant for our fall, God changed it all for the good of us, the human creation, that we may find Him and know Him. He is the only One who can save you and me from the hand of the enemy. Because everything was only made for Him and through Him, the Lord Jesus. (See John 1:3.) **He is the only Saviour, the only One who has the power to save us.** Why did our Lord die on the Cross for us? So that the Spirit of every man could live forever, guaranteeing our spirit man will be alive with Him; in accordance with His Word and our expectation that we will live with Him, because we accepted that

He is our Lord, and Saviour, the Living One and alive forevermore, the only Rescuer now and forever.

Do not obey the enemy or you'll be forever dead or spiritually comatose under his painful unquenchable fire in hell—because he will be forever there, with you in tow, if you don't believe Jesus' word.

If we would just only die physically and we didn't have a spirit worth rescuing, then the Lord Jesus died for nothing. (So Easter is kaput, and Christmas!) And if that is so, why, after over two thousand years, are there still those people who believe? You know why? They are still experiencing the power of God in their lives—fact! But God knows that every living being has a spirit—He gave it to us—that's worth rescuing. You have a choice: heaven or hell, both real. God placed a point of contact with us, putting His only begotten Son to physical death in place of our spirit's death.

The Lord Jesus has now placed in our hands the decision to accept Him with His invitation to rescue our living soul and spirit, but we have to make the decision individually. **Even if our parents are Christians, we cannot inherit their Christianity or salvation.** We can only make up our own minds to accept Him and His sacrificial love for us through His death on the Cross of Calvary for us to have eternal life. He was and is and will be the only Saviour. He is the Host in heaven for all souls and men's spirits.

In the book of Acts 1:1–11 (after the Lord Jesus rose from the dead) it says: *In my former book, Theophilus, I wrote about all that Jesus began to do and to teach until the day He was taken up to heaven, **after giving instructions through the Holy Spirit** to the apostles He had chosen. After His suffering, He presented Himself to them and **gave many convincing proofs that He was alive**. He appeared to them over a period of forty days and spoke about the kingdom of God. On one occasion, while he was eating with them, he gave them this command: "Do not leave Jerusalem, but **wait for the gift My Father promised**, which you have heard Me speak about. For John baptised with water, but in a few days **you will be baptised with the Holy Spirit**."*

Then they gathered round him and asked him, "Lord, are you at this time going to restore the kingdom to Israel?"

*He said to them: "It is not for you to know the times or dates the Father has set by His own authority. But **you will receive power when the Holy Spirit comes on you**; and you will be My witnesses in Jerusalem, and in all Judea and Samaria, and to the ends of the earth."*

After He said this, He was taken up before their very eyes, and a cloud hid Him from their sight.

They were looking intently up into the sky as He was going, when suddenly two men dressed in white stood beside them. "Men of Galilee," they said, "why do you stand here looking into the sky? This same Jesus, who has been taken from you into heaven, will come back in the same way you have seen Him go into heaven."

Everything that exists today—in heaven, on earth, under the earth, principalities, powers, dominions, kingdoms visible and invisible—was created for the Lord Jesus and through Him (see Colossians 1:16–18). Anyone who claims anything different from God's Word is not telling the truth; there's only one true GOD and there's only One Son of God: His name, as you know, is JESUS.

The Lord Jesus is the only One who can complete you.

9

THE LORD JESUS IS PREPARING A MANSION FOR YOU IN HEAVEN

When the Lord Jesus invites you to His party (Salvation or Recognition Party, as I call it), to be a part of His plan and be in His will, He doesn't expect you to do any work; He is just asking you to come, come as you are. And He would not invite you if you did not have a place to stay; He was preparing a place for you a long time ago—a mansion, yes, a mansion.... There's a mansion waiting for you and me in heaven; for Jesus said in John 14:2–3: *"In My Father's house are many mansions; if it were not so, I would have told you. I go to prepare a place for you. And if I go and prepare a place for you, **I will come again and receive you to Myself***; *that where I Am there you may be also."*

"Well," you might say, "I don't want a mansion next to Naylee in heaven." Sorry man, you haven't got any choice which mansion the Lord Jesus will put you in, so make sure you don't have any hard feelings towards other people on earth. Oh, I just remembered, you cannot be there if you have never forgiven from your heart all your enemies; we will all be brothers and sisters in heaven.

So do you think you would like to come to this place of no sickness and no crying—where it will be peaceful, serene, and full of grace and songs of praise and joy? You'll never be lonely there. We would be free to eat from the tree of life, when we overcome the world by the blood of the Lamb and word of our testimony; see Revelation 2:7 and Revelation 12:11.

If you refuse to believe the Word of Jesus in the Bible (God's word is correct and I'm trying to copy it for you) there will be gnashing of teeth in the fire of hell—and hell is for real. It says in John 3:18 that a person is condemned already if they do not believe in the Son of God. Also, in Psalm 9:17 it says: ***The wicked shall be turned into hell, and all the nations that forget God.*** So remember, the Saviour of the world is alive today and is waiting for your response. He wants to have a relationship with you to enable you to come to Him without any barrier, emotionally, or anything to hide from Him. He wants you to be yourself in His company.

In Luke 12:5 the Lord Jesus is speaking to those who are listening to Him from this passage: (This is the Lord Jesus' warning to all!) *"But I will show you whom you should fear:* ***fear Him who, after He has killed, has power to cast into hell;*** *yes, I say to you, fear Him!* So it's a no brainer really. If you refuse to believe God or even to refuse to believe that there is hell, what is your basis that hell does not exist? Even the Lord Jesus Himself mentioned it in the Bible (His Testimony!), because both places (heaven and hell) clearly exist.

There's no fleshly being (mortal man) who could become immortal without God's transforming power over him, and the **immortal beings can't go back and become mortal again.** What I am trying to say here is, no Angels could become mortal. That's why the angels who disobeyed God could never be redeemed any longer—by the Lord Jesus' death and resurrection power or by God—for they are already immortal, living forever. They already knew right from wrong when they were created.

Did you know that the Angels will be judged too? See 1 Corinthians 6:3: *Do you not know that we will judge angels? How much more the things of this life!* According to this passage we will judge the Angels. I would not know how to do that and I did not see their hearts, but through God their motives will be exposed, maybe? When we die, no other power apart from that of the living God, who transformed Jesus' body when God raised Him from the dead, has any power over all and above our spirit man. **No one can detain or hold onto their spirit and soul after they die; once our spirit leaves our body, it's an irrecoverable process.** It is actually an automatic process of transformation from being in the physical (man's nature), to the spiritual, by God's decision.

All men were warned over and over again through the Word of God to believe God, and not take Jesus for granted, nor His teaching and His Word lightly, because the consequences of it all are unpardonable, especially when you blaspheme the Holy Spirit. It is said the blasphemy against the Lord Jesus will be pardoned but the blasphemy against the Holy Spirit will not be pardoned, either in life here or in life everlasting. So be very careful with your mouth, what you speak of. In Matthew 12:32 it says: ***Anyone who speaks a word against the Son of Man will be forgiven, but anyone who speaks against the Holy Spirit will not be forgiven, either in this age or in the age to come.*** (You see, there is the age to come.)

Hell was not intended for human beings.

Hell was not created for humans, but for the fallen angels; because they were created spiritually discerned and created (immortal) higher than human beings. Remember what it says in Isaiah 55:9: *For as the heavens are higher than the earth so My ways are higher than your ways, and My thoughts than your thoughts.* And these fallen Angels were created higher than us; these are the inhabitants of one of the Lord's heavens.

It says in Matthew 25:41: *"Then He will also say to those on the left hand, 'Depart from Me, you cursed, into the everlasting fire **prepared for the devil and his angels**.* So you see, the devil has his own fallen angels with him. These are the angels who didn't obey God. They will be thrown into hell; and if the angels could be thrown into hell, how much more a human who does not even believe and acknowledge God—**even the devil believed God and shuddered!** See James 2:19. When the Lord Jesus keeps on saying to believe Him, He is not joking!

And there are also created things under the earth, who bow down at the authority of the Lord Jesus' name; for it says in Philippians 2:10: *that at the name of Jesus every knee should bow, of those in heaven, and of those on earth, and of those under the earth.* We do not know what the Lord created under the earth, but even those under the earth are also subject to Jesus' name. ***All things were created through Him*** (**Jesus**) ***and for Him***.

The Lord Jesus said, *"Believe Me when I say that I am in the Father and the Father is in Me; or at least believe on the evidence of the works themselves"*(John 14:11).

The works the Lord Jesus is talking about are the miracles He did while He was on earth with His disciples. He did a few miracles in His time, and the first miracle he did was turning the water into wine. His mother Mary, and His disciples were all invited to the wedding at Cana in Galilee. When the host of the wedding banquet had run out of wine, Mary His mother told Jesus, and in response to her request the Lord Jesus turned the water into wine. See John 2:1–11.

Here are some more miracles of Jesus:

Jesus Heals a Man Born Blind

John 9:1–12: *As He went along, He saw a man blind from birth. His disciples asked him, "Rabbi, who sinned, this man or his parents, that he was born blind?" "Neither this man nor his parents sinned," said Jesus, "but this happened so that the works of God might be displayed in him. As long as it is day, we must do the works of him who sent me. Night is coming, when no one can work. While I am in the world, I am the light of the world."*
After saying this, he spit on the ground, made some mud with the saliva, and put it on the man's eyes. "Go," he told him, "wash in the Pool of Siloam" (this word means "Sent"). So the man went and washed, and came home seeing.
His neighbours and those who had formerly seen him begging asked, "Isn't this the same man who used to sit and beg?" Some claimed that he was.
Others said, "No, he only looks like him."
But he himself insisted, "I am the man."
"How then were your eyes opened?" they asked.
He replied, "The man they call Jesus made some mud and put it on my eyes. He told me to go to Siloam and wash. So I went and washed, and then I could see."
"Where is this man?" they asked him.
"I don't know," he said.

The Healing at the Pool

John 5:1–14: *Some time later, Jesus went up to Jerusalem for one of the Jewish festivals. Now there is in Jerusalem near the*

THE LORD JESUS IS PREPARING A MANSION FOR YOU IN HEAVEN

Sheep Gate a pool, which in Aramaic is called Bethesda and which is surrounded by five covered colonnades. Here a great number of disabled people used to lie—the blind, the lame, the paralyzed. One who was there had been an invalid for thirty-eight years. When Jesus saw him lying there and learned that he had been in this condition for a long time, He asked him, "Do you want to get well?"

"Sir," the invalid replied, "I have no one to help me into the pool when the water is stirred. While I am trying to get in, someone else goes down ahead of me."

Then Jesus said to him, "Get up! Pick up your mat and walk." At once the man was cured; he picked up his mat and walked.

The day on which this took place was a Sabbath, and so the Jewish leaders said to the man who had been healed, "It is the Sabbath; the law forbids you to carry your mat."

But he replied, "The man who made me well said to me, 'Pick up your mat and walk.' " So they asked him, "Who is this fellow who told you to pick it up and walk?"

The man who was healed had no idea who it was, for Jesus had slipped away into the crowd that was there.

Later Jesus found him at the temple and said to him, "See, you are well again. Stop sinning or something worse may happen to you." The man went away and told the Jewish leaders that it was Jesus who had made him well.

Jesus Raises Lazarus From the Dead

John 11:38–44: *Jesus, once more deeply moved, came to the tomb. It was a cave with a stone laid across the entrance. "Take away the stone," he said.*

"But, Lord," said Martha, the sister of the dead man, "by this time there is a bad odour, for he has been there four days."

Then Jesus said, "Did I not tell you that if you believe, you will see the glory of God?"

So they took away the stone. Then Jesus looked up and said, "Father, I thank you that you have heard me. I knew that you always hear me, but I said this for the benefit of the people standing here, that they may believe that you sent me."

When he had said this, Jesus called in a loud voice, "Lazarus, come out!" The dead man came out, his hands and feet wrapped with strips of linen, and a cloth around his face.
Jesus said to them, "Take off the grave clothes and let him go."
These are just a few examples of the Lord Jesus' miracles.

I've read, heard and seen on television that there are some people who have experienced life after death. A few of them have said that the grass in Paradise is so green, and that when you step on it, it goes back upright as it was. So it seems things in heaven do not get damaged.

Ian Mac Cormack, a New Zealander who was stung by deadly box jellyfish while diving in Mauritius died and went to heaven. He experienced wave after wave of—as he described it—God's 'liquid love' being poured out into him, which he couldn't contain. He saw written in space words from the Bible, and the Lord's prayer. After some time, the Lord showed him a glimpse of eternity, and the Lord asked him if he wanted to stay in heaven or to return to earth. He was thinking to himself that he had no wife or children to leave behind, and no mortgage to pay either, so he could stay in heaven.

But then God showed him his mother, who was praying for his salvation at that time, and if he stayed in heaven then his mum wouldn't know that he had now got saved. It would upset her so much and it might weaken her faith.

And by the grace of God, the Lord enabled him to return to his body in the bed where he was lying in the morgue, to tell his story to the whole world. And I was so privileged to hear and see it on film. A fantastic testimony.

I had a dream when I was little (and I know the Lord speaks to His people in dreams and visions), that I went to this place where I realised in my dream was heaven, because the place was really serene and peaceful, and there was no conversation involving speaking, but only thoughts, which was speech to anyone I wanted to have a conversation with. There wouldn't be any shouting in heaven. There was no sun there but it was bright, and the light in that place wouldn't burn you. So I knew it really was Heaven.

THE LORD JESUS IS PREPARING A MANSION FOR YOU IN HEAVEN

So Father God does not want anyone to be away from Him and the Lord Jesus, but since you have a choice, you need to make the right decision for yourself. Do not go on what the majority of people choose just because you think there's a lot of them so they must be right.

Who in these other religions like Buddhist, Hindu and even so called Christian science can offer you eternal life or promise you a mansion in heaven, the place of repose for your soul? When you see an epitaph on a gravestone, quite often you see the words 'Rest in Peace'. But if your soul doesn't have peace when you die then it would be an everlasting unrest for your soul.

You can only rest in the mansion the Lord Jesus has for you when you become acquainted with Him, and have a personal relationship with Him. It says in 2 Corinthians 5:17–21: *Therefore, if anyone is in Christ, the new creation has come: The old has gone, the new is here! All this is from God, who reconciled us to himself through Christ and gave us the ministry of reconciliation: that God was reconciling the world to himself in Christ, not counting people's sins against them. And he has committed to us the **message of reconciliation**. We are therefore Christ's ambassadors, as though God were making his appeal through us. We implore you on Christ's behalf: Be reconciled to God. God made him who had no sin to be sin for us, so that in him we might become the righteousness of God.*

Have you ever heard of any human who came back to life after three days in the grave, apart from the Lord Jesus or at the will of God? I have never heard of any yet, but there is nothing impossible with God. What's the point of coming back to this life here anyway, if you are already dead? If you're a Christian you're resting in the Paradise of God. If you don't believe in Jesus you can't come back anyway, even if you want to, unless the Lord Jesus allows you. It only makes me think about this because when the Lord Jesus was talking to His disciples about John the Baptist, who had been beheaded, He was implying that the spirit of John the Baptist was Elijah's, see Matthew 17:10–13. By the way, Elijah didn't die; he was taken on a chariot of fire to heaven. When the people searched for his body, no one could find him, the Lord had taken him.

Even when Elisha was telling Elijah's servants not to look for him, they insisted on looking for Elijah. To stop Elisha from feeling embarrassed for them, he told them to search for him, his master Elijah, but he knew he wouldn't be found on earth. And he was right. See 1Kings 2:1–18.

Are you still not convinced? I cannot do anything to convince you, but may the Holy Spirit convict you of your stubborn unbelief, Amen.

If you allow the Lord Jesus into your heart, He will let you into your mansion in heaven, which He is preparing for you.

10

ARE YOU COMING TO GOD'S PARTY? YOU ARE INVITED

God's invitation is for real and there is an urgency in His command. It says in the book of John 6:44: *"No one can come to Me unless the Father who sent Me draws them, and I will raise them up at the last day."* (The Lord Jesus has promised you will be with Him.) So come to Him with an honest heart, you whom He values, adores and loves. Our souls and spirits are treasured by God. He foreknew us and created us in His very own image, you who are the apple of His eye, you whom Jesus lovingly and tenderly cares for. Look unto Him who knows you are in need of Him. You may not discern it or feel it, but the Lord Jesus knows you need Him in your life, here on earth and in everlasting life.

Come to Him, you who do not know where life stirs you; come into the midst of the people who know God, and the power of His might. Come into the presence of the congregation where God's peace dwells and love for each other exists. Come to that church whose hearts beat for God and His people. Be a part of that family of believers. Sit and mingle with them and your peace will be overflowing.

I know a lot of people are thirsty for affection, love, and connection with others. The Lord gave us these emotions because these feelings exist in Him as we are made in His likeness.

The Lord is offering us a solution for our everyday life. We carry all our problems in our minds—when we worry, and in our soul—when we do not have peace, and in our hearts—when we feel empty or have inner pain—even physical pain. That's when we are carrying too much of a burden. And it's not in our actual physical heads, but in our minds; not in our actual souls, but in our emotions; not on our actual shoulders, but the tiredness and heaviness of everyday life in our heart. It makes us tired of the everyday grind of work, and of people and life itself.

Your spirit—'the inner you'—receives the peace of heart and

mind and joy in your soul that you can only get from God. God's burden is easy—His Spirit makes our spirit-man lighter emotionally. A calling on Jesus, a closing of our eyes to cut out the world, is like closing our front door to the public and people we are close to. **The Lord wants you to have a 'me time' with Him.** Your 'me time' with Him means sitting comfortably, asking the Holy Spirit to be with you and inviting Him to bring peace to your heart, and quieting your soul before Him. Tell Him all that makes you feel heavy—work, people and life itself. Wait for the Holy Spirit to bring His peace to you.

You may be saying to yourself, "How could I go to God? Would He hear me or even listen to me?" It says in Psalm 34:18: *The Lord is close to the broken hearted and saves those who are crushed in spirit,* so only through prayers and supplication can you come to Him. You might be thinking, "I've never prayed before," and feel such a hypocrite for asking for God's help now. But this is the right time to ask Him. For Him, asking for His help is not hypocritical but it's humbling yourself before Him who has the power over you and your circumstances. And the best thing as well is to ask Him to guide and lead you in your everyday life. You might say, "But how?" Ask Him to help you be in tune with the Holy Spirit, who will come and live in your heart, to guide and lead you forever.

The Lord Jesus' invitation never goes out of date. There is **no** specific time or season or **expiry date** while you are still living on earth. It would never be over until the day you leave this planet earth, or when the Lord Jesus returns for the second time. Then it might be too late for you, if you don't act now. Life is short and you never know when your time is up, so now is the right time to consider Jesus' invitation. In Matthew 4:17 we read: *From that time Jesus began to preach and to say,* **"Repent, for the kingdom of heaven is at hand."**

"So what do I have to do and to know before I could accept the Lord Jesus' invitation? What is this party, and what is there to celebrate, and why am I invited?" you may ask. You have to come because one day you will die; this is everyone's final destiny, and you are invited because you are alive today. I call it the 'welcome home party'—as you've been away for a while.

The Lord Jesus didn't want heaven empty; He actually

wanted us to be with Him in heaven. For this is what He said in John 17:24: *"Father, I desire that they also whom You gave Me may **be with Me where I am**, that they may behold My glory which You have given Me; for You loved Me before the foundation of the world."*

The earth could not come up to heaven, so heaven came down to earth, through the Lord Jesus.

There's a worship song called 'What a Beautiful Name'—it means Jesus' name. In verse two of this song it goes: *You didn't want heaven without us, so Jesus, You brought heaven down.* This part of the song brought comfort to me when my sister was very ill. When I was praying to the Lord to send His angel to my sister's hospital bed, I saw the Lord Jesus in a vision walking in the hospital room where my sister was and He was sitting on the chair waiting for her to wake up.

I felt the Lord give me this scripture: *Our God is the God of salvation; and to God the Lord belong escapes from death* (Psalm 68:20). I took this verse that my sister was going to get healed. But in the end she didn't. I even said to one of the ladies in my church, "The Lord Jesus didn't send His Angel to my sister's hospital bed; He Himself came waiting for her to wake up."

When the Lord Jesus came to earth, He brought heaven down to us. This is so, so true with His Word in the scripture, when He said, *"I come that you may have life and have it more abundantly."* He brought Himself down to earth, to save us to be with Him in this 'Welcome Home Party' in heaven, as I call it.

I knew my sister was saved, otherwise the Lord wouldn't have waited for her to wake up from her sleep and take her home. I felt comforted that the Lord had taken her with Him.

I did have a sense that my sister was still going to recover, as I took 'escapes from death' to refer to natural death. But one time when my husband and I were worshipping at home, I was speaking in tongues and bitterly grieving in spirit, which gave me the sense my sister would die. But I still insisted in my mind that she would live, because of the escapes from death scripture. So when she died I realised then that it was spiritual death she had escaped from. So I thank You, Lord Jesus, for saving my sister's life from the second death. I know I will see her in heaven when my time comes to end on earth.

And it also brings comfort to me that my sister's life was lent to us by God. We have enjoyed her company, her sense of humour, her kind heart, and good character towards us all. I would like to say she is my best sister, but my other sisters are good to me as well. And I know everyone's life will end and all will return to God who gave it.

My sister didn't accept the Lord Jesus in her heart, as far as I know, before she became really ill. But I wasn't always with her and I sent her a few of the 'Word for Today' daily readings a few times and at the end of that booklet there's a salvation prayer. I don't know if she ever prayed that, but all I know was the Lord Jesus visited her in her hospital bed and waited for her to wake up so that He could take her home, to heaven. And the Lord Jesus doesn't want heaven without us, that's why He came down and brought heaven down to us. Mortal men cannot go to heaven so the immortal God came down to us on earth and redeemed us so we can be with Him in heaven.

The Lord Jesus will not disappoint me; I know my sister will be with Him in heaven. It brings comfort to me that everyone has been given the chance to be with Him. His perfect will for us is to be so close to Him and to be happy to be with Him in heaven. He created our spirit within; for Him to dwell in our spiritual being. *God is Spirit, and those who worship Him must worship in spirit and truth* (John 4:24).

His loving kindness will never fail. So for those who are already believers, do not lose hope; pray for your unsaved loved ones because God answers prayers if they are offered to Him from your heart. Let him who comes to God come to Him with reverence and hope, for His everlasting love will never end, as long as you obey His Words. His loving kindness is everlasting; He will never be able to disown you when you come to Him.

I realised according to Acts 28:22–27 that the hardening of people's heart and ears was a sort of spiritual illness which needed to be healed, as it says in these verses (this was the Jews talking to apostle Paul): *But we want to hear what your views are, for we know that people everywhere are talking against this* sect." They arranged to meet Paul on a certain day, and came in even larger numbers to the place where he was staying. He witnessed to them from morning till evening, explaining about the kingdom of God, and from the Law of Moses and from the Prophets he tried to persuade them about Jesus. Some were convinced by what he said, but others would not believe. They disagreed among themselves and began to leave after Paul had made this final statement: "**The Holy Spirit spoke the truth** to your ancestors when he said through Isaiah the prophet:

"'Go to this people and say, "You will be ever hearing but never understanding; you will be ever seeing but never perceiving." For this people's heart has become calloused; they hardly hear with their ears, and they have closed their eyes. Otherwise they might see with their eyes, hear with their ears, understand with their hearts **and turn, and I would heal them.**'

On the death of the Lord Jesus when He said "It is finished," He truly provided us with everything we need for our salvation, including healing our senses: eyes to see, ears to hear, and hearts to understand His message for our salvation. On His death the veil at the Temple was torn from top to bottom; that signifies that we can now come closer to God. It wasn't possible before His death, but now that all the barriers were down between God and us through Jesus' sacrifice, it brings us closer to our Redeemer (Matt 27:51) to have a personal relationship with Him.

When God created the heavens and the things we can see, like the moon and stars and the sun and clouds, lightning and thunder, and sometimes rainbows as well, these are the things we are permitted to know and see. But according to Paul, one of the apostles, he was taken up to the third heaven and he saw things that he was not permitted to tell on earth, see 2 Corinthians 12: 1–4: *Although there is nothing to be gained, I will go on to visions and revelations from the Lord. I know a man in Christ who fourteen years ago **was caught up to the third heaven**. Whether it was **in the body or out of the body** I do not know— God knows. And I know that this man—whether in the body or apart from the body I do not know, but God knows—**was caught up to paradise and heard inexpressible things, things that no one is permitted to tell**.*

Some people who have experienced being in heaven have a

barrier of not allowing them to tell everything they've seen and heard. So you see, heaven wasn't empty and God wasn't lonely. And there are secrets in the heavens that we are not allowed to know yet while we are on earth.

The angels were there and they were executors of God's words, and were also considered as the sons of God, until one of the angels left his domain and interrupted and tempted the woman in the Garden of Eden. I am so convinced that this angel transgressed before any humans ever did; otherwise he wouldn't have been at his business of tempting the woman.

If you remember, after Cain sinned he went to the land of Nod, East of the Garden of Eden—where the Lord placed cherubim to guard the way to the tree of life, and **he found a wife there**—see Genesis 4:16–17. Where on earth did she come from? Did his parents have other children in the Garden of Eden? It's only recorded that Abel and Cain were present with their parents. This made my inquisitive thoughts wave through thinking about Genesis 4:13–17: *Cain said to the Lord, "My punishment is more than I can bear. Today You are driving me from the land and I will be hidden from Your presence; I will be a restless wanderer on the earth and whoever finds me will kill me."* (If only Adam and Eve were living on the earth at that time, **who would find him and kill him**?) *Then the lord put a mark on Cain **so that no one who found him would kill him**. So Cain went out from the Lord's presence and **lived in the land of Nod, east of Eden**. Cain **lay with his wife**, and she became pregnant and gave birth to Enoch. Cain was then building a city* (building a city? It means the east of the Garden of Eden was inhabited by other people, when he was living there) *and he named it after his son Enoch.*

A woman I know at work said Cain married his sister and it was incest. I believe she has never even fully read the Bible. But Adam and Eve were created, not conceived. Adam was moulded from the ground while Eve was taken out of Adam's rib; so they were not born of one parent. She just thought of the natural system of conception, but the God I know is a Super Natural God. Eve could not have a trail of blood each month—they didn't even have a stitch on. Periods, I believe, were one of the direct consequences of their sin. In Genesis 3:16 God said to the woman: *"I will greatly multiply your sorrow and **your conception**; in pain you shall bring forth children; your desire shall be for your husband, and he shall rule over you."* As we know, if a woman doesn't have periods she cannot conceive!

Cain's wife came from the east of Eden where Adam and Eve had been driven out. Can you see that Cain himself wanted to go back to the place where the first sin was committed by his fleshly parents? If I could be allowed to speculate, did Adam and Eve leave some children in the east of the Garden of Eden? Did those children they left not sin directly, before Adam and Eve sinned? Were they referred to as 'the sons of God', and they sinned eventually? For it says in Ezekiel 18:4: *"Behold, all souls are Mine; the soul of the father as well as the soul of the son is Mine; **the soul who sins shall die.**"* So if they didn't disobey God's commands at that time, and only their parents sinned, then they probably weren't driven away from the Garden of Eden. Were these children in the Garden known as the sons (and daughters) of God? It always says sons of God, but Cain got a wife there, a woman, a daughter....

Now in Genesis 6:1–2 & 4–8 it says: *Now it came to pass, when men began to multiply on the face of the earth, and daughters were born to them, that **the sons of God** saw the daughters of men, that they were beautiful; and they took wives for themselves of all whom they chose. There were giants on the earth in those days, and also afterward, when **the sons of God came in to the daughters of men and they bore children to them**. Those were the mighty men who were of old, men of renown.* It is clearly stated their offspring were giants; those born of divine beings—sons of God, and daughters of men—human beings, and they were wicked people, **every inclination of their hearts was continually evil and grieved the heart of God.** *So the Lord said, "I will destroy man whom I have created from the face of the earth, both man and beast, creeping things and birds of the air, for I am sorry that I have made them." But Noah found grace in the eyes of the Lord.* Thank You, Lord, for Noah.

My first point is that humans sinned. But who was this tempter? The fallen Angel who was created as an overseer in the Garden of Eden, where everyone including sons and daughters of God had to be looked after, was a covering cherub. Why was there a covering cherub then? Why did the inhabitants of the Garden need a covering cherub? Is it true to think that some angels had already sinned? It says in Ezekiel 28:12–19: *"Son of man, take up a lamentation for the king of Tyre, and say to him, 'Thus says the Lord God:*

"You were the seal of perfection, full of wisdom and perfect in beauty. **You were in Eden, the garden of God.** **"You were the anointed cherub who covers; I established you; you were on the holy mountain of God;** *you walked back and forth in the midst of fiery stones. You were perfect in your ways from the day you were created, till iniquity was found in you.*

"Your heart was lifted up because of your beauty; you corrupted your wisdom for the sake of your splendour; I cast you to the ground, I laid you before kings, that they might gaze at you.

"You defiled your sanctuaries by the multitude of your iniquities, by the iniquity of your trading; therefore I brought fire from your midst; it devoured you, and I turned you to ashes upon the earth in the sight of all who saw you. All who knew you among the peoples are astonished at you; you have become a horror, and shall be no more forever.'"

As he became a walking angel on earth, God destroyed him. This angel was in the Garden of Eden, that's why he managed to tempt and deceive both Adam and Eve to eat from the tree of the knowledge of good and evil. He sinned before Adam and Eve sinned, otherwise he could not have tempted them to eat of the fruit that made them know right from wrong, good and evil. The devil was created first—before any human was created—and he wasn't created as a devil but as a covering angel! The angels that left their domain sinned and will be judged. **When angels sinned they became devils**; after humans sinned we became spiritually dead, cut off from God. Jesus became human for humans' sake, so Jesus could take us up to His Father, a Spirit God. It would be our spirit man that the Lord Jesus will take up to His Father, our God, so we could be a spirit being before God.

The Lord Jesus always emphasizes **He was sent by His Father**, and we Christians believe Him and His Word. He is the Mediator; without the Mediator—no life everlasting for us.

When Adam and Eve sinned and were thrown out of the

Garden with their due punishment, fear gripped their hearts, see Genesis 3:8–10. They hid themselves from God, and yes, their (natural) eyes were opened and they saw themselves naked! The devil opened the human senses in them. The devil, who was supposed to be a covering angel, created divine, above humans, had become corrupt and defiled himself. When the Lord God said to the serpent, *"I will put enmity between you and the woman, and between your seed and her **Seed**; He shall bruise your head, and you shall bruise His heel,"* the angels of God were thrown out of the Garden together with Adam and Eve. Note that this king of Tyre was known as one of the angels in the Garden of God.

Was there any living being in the garden before the fall of man? I don't want to speculate but after the Lord created the woman He commanded them to be fruitful and multiply—and when the Lord speaks the word, things come into existence. Her SEED is the Lord Jesus, who crushed the head of the serpent a few thousand years later. **And we are the children of her SEED if we are believers in Christ, so we too could crush the enemy's head under our feet**. For greater is He who is in me and you than he who is in the world, see 1 John 4:4.

And through what I understand in this passage, would it be possible to say that when the devil was thrown down to earth, he ruled on earth as god?

'Therefore thus says the Lord God: "Because you have set your heart as the heart of a god, behold, therefore, I will bring strangers against you, the most terrible of the nations; and they shall draw their swords against the beauty of your wisdom, and defile your splendour. They shall throw you down into the Pit, and you shall die the death of the slain in the midst of the seas.

"Will you still say before him who slays you, 'I am a god'? ***But you shall be a man, and not a god****, in the hand of him who slays you. You shall die the death of the uncircumcised by the hand of aliens; for I have spoken," says the Lord God.'"* See Ezekiel 28.

That is his first punishment, the second is to come, and no forgiveness for him because he was an angel, created a holy being! God cast him out. He was supposed to be a covering angel for the humans lacking knowledge. When the Lord Jesus created humans in God's image, it didn't say we were created perfect; but the angels were created perfect. A spirit with an immortal body, an invisible being, but they could make themselves visible to us, as overseers of humans, I believe.

Because this fallen angel thought he was like God, he ruled on earth, and as it was, there was trading going on, so corruption and pride and boasting ruled the hearts of man and those of half-angel half-man—who were still humans as giants, but not gods.

God didn't say He created humans in perfection, but according to this passage in Ezekiel this fallen angel was perfect in beauty and was a guardian cherub in the Garden of Eden, and walked along freely in the mountain of God. But he became arrogant and proud of his position twinned with his pride, because of his beauty and wisdom and success. He crashed down with such a great big bang on earth.

If the angel sinned before Adam and Eve did, God knew Adam and Eve would sin too; it would only be a matter of time. That's why the tree of the knowledge of good and evil and the tree of life were placed in the garden as God's testing objects.

This is what it says in Deuteronomy 13:3: *For the Lord your God is testing you to know whether you love the Lord your God with all your heart and with all your soul.* You might say, why then, did God expect us to be obedient to Him? Because there are still other angels that are very obedient to God's purpose and will to this day. So God truly was so gracious to us and gave us a choice to stand and believe with Him. God so loved us, so He gave us freewill; **if God did not give us a choice, that is not love.** The Lord said in Genesis 2:16: *"You are free to eat from any tree in the garden* (a choice, freewill*); but you must not eat from the tree of the knowledge of good and evil."* If we didn't have any freewill we would be like robots who would obey everything God commanded us to do. God created us as beings with feelings, because He is a God who feels pain, jealousy, sadness and anger. Jesus even wept, just like we do. This freedom we achieved since knowing good and bad made us responsible for our own will, and we became lovers of ourselves (this was predicted long before it happened) see 2 Timothy 3:2: *For people will love only themselves and their money. They will be boastful and proud,* **scoffing at God***, disobedient to their* *parents, and ungrateful.* **They will consider nothing sacred.**

Though Adam and Eve sinned, God didn't curse them; **God cursed the earth, and God cursed the snake, but God did not curse humans; He clothed them instead.** It was only after the first man and woman sinned that sickness became present in the life of all human beings—a product of disobedience.

Maybe that old snake thought, "Ah, if I could tempt the parents, then I could tempt all the children too. The whole human creation will fall for me." And yes, we fell. I'm glad that God put enmity between us and the devil; it means the Lord Jesus had already agreed with His Father, our God, to rescue us from the devil's wiles. When God said, I will put enmity between your seed—the devil's offspring, the follower of the snake—and **her Seed—that Seed is the Lord Jesus**—God was telling the devil that humans will have authority over him. Those who believe in Jesus as the Messiah will crush the serpent's head. This means, as followers of Christ Jesus, we have now obtained authority over our enemy, by the power of His Name. The Lord Jesus gave us the Power in His Name to use against the devil. All believers have that Power and the Authority of Jesus Christ of Nazareth's Name over our enemy!

Now the Lord Jesus, born to live under the law, given by God to Moses on the Mount Sinai, **lived under His own law—the human law**—died under the human law and was the only One sinless in the sight of God. Our Lord **Jesus lived under and observed the law of the earth He created**, so that **He mingled** with the people He created; yet **He honoured** and revered **Father God** by offering Himself to die on the Cross of Calvary—having all the human qualities yet God—for the redemption of human souls. In Him **the divine and the mortal fused together.**

He was welcomed by Mary His mother, when she said, "Be it unto me according to **Your Word**." So **Mary** obeyed God and **dethroned her own will** and **enthroned Father God's will** from her heart, when she accepted the will of God to be the mother of the Messiah. Jesus was born not of the will of man but **of the will of God**—see John 1:13.

The Lord Jesus could only come down from heaven if no human hand had touched the tree of life, otherwise we would live forever sinful, like the fallen angels who disobeyed God. God placed a guardian Angel to guard the way to the tree of life, **and preserve humanity from hell**. When God said to *Fill the earth and subdue it, to rule over the fish of the sea, the birds of the air and all that moves and creeps on the face of the ground*, that was the clue that they would sin. **If they would only have to stay in the Garden** of Eden **they wouldn't need to subdue anything on earth**. Then they wouldn't even be given any instruction about the earth. Since the angels, who are higher in wisdom and have power and authority over humans, sinned, God knew that we too would sin. God was not scared that men would fall, or that some angels would sin.

God saw something in Abraham's heart that He knew He could build him up and they (the Israelites) would listen to Him. It was not the righteous or upright things Abraham and his predecessors did, but God is faithful.

When God made the promise to Abraham, **since God could swear by no one greater, He swore by Himself**, *and said: "By Myself I have sworn, says the Lord, because you have done this thing, and have not withheld your son, your only son—blessing I will bless you, and multiplying I will multiply your descendants as the stars of the heaven and as the sand which is on the seashore; and your descendants shall possess the gate of their enemies* (Genesis 22:16–17).

This son mentioned here was Isaac the child who would produce children as numerous as the sand on the seashore. It's seems so unreal that God would ask Abraham to kill his only son and offer him on the Altar as a sacrifice for God. You see, He tests people; He look at the integrity of the heart.

Everything the Lord God promises, He does. He said He will walk with His Prophets, and His disciples, He will strengthen them and save them from the hands of the enemy. For God looks at the heart of man. They only became enemies to God because they forsook God and served and worshipped other gods, which is not God at all.

God's purpose in us is to impress upon our minds and hearts His desire **to hold on to our hope in Him** and not to drift away into false hopes offered by the world. He said to be content with what you have.

And I do believe the Garden of Eden will not be found anywhere on earth now; it was never on earth in the first place, it was always higher than the earth. It is now the Paradise of God, a resting place for the souls of those who died revering and honouring God. **We can eat fruit from the tree of life**, but we have to overcome the devil. In Revelation 2:7 it says: *He who has an ear let him hear what the Spirit says to the churches. To him who overcomes* (the lies of the enemy and acknowledges Jesus' authority over the enemy) *I will give to* **eat** *from* **the tree of life, which is in the midst of the Paradise of God.** (The Garden of Eden is the Paradise of God which is now in heaven.)

Don't seek the earth or you will be thrown out of it to hell. Seek heaven with me and the rest of our Christians families. **Our Saviour is there, waiting for us to occupy the mansion he's preparing for us.** Both angels and humans have freewill but the Angel of God has higher responsibility than us.

In Psalms 91:13–16: *You shall tread upon the lion and the cobra, the young lion and* **the serpent you shall trample underfoot***. Because* **he has set his love upon Me, therefore I will deliver him; I will set him on high because he has known My Name. I will be with him in trouble. I will deliver him and honour him***. With long life I will satisfy him and show him My salvation.* You will trample the lion, the snake (the one who incited Eve to sin) and the scorpions (his little demons) in the Name of Jesus Christ of Nazareth, for we know the truth and stand and believe His Word from our heart and mind. **You could never trample underfoot what was higher than you**, but always the ones below you!

From the beginning of the world the Lord Jesus has defeated the devil, through the Word of God—so use God's Word. When the devil tempted Him, the **Lord Jesus said, "It is written."**

The **unbelievers** don't respond to God; **their hearts and minds are closed to God**, their spirit is far and disobedient to God, see Matthew 13:15: *For the hearts of this people have grown dull. Their ears are hard of hearing, and their eyes they have closed, Lest they should see with their eyes and hear with their ears, Lest they should understand with their hearts and turn, So that I should heal them.* In James 2:26 it says: *'The body without the spirit is dead, so faith without work is dead also.'*

Our spirit needs to be awakened by the Word of the Living God. **Jesus is the Author of all Life.**

My final point is: **No one was born of his own will, everyone comes from the Lord Jesus.** You didn't choose God, but He chose you and He loved you before you knew sinning. God also chose your race and place of birth, and to whom were you to be born. He equipped you for life, but you need to search what God has placed in you.

In the beginning was the Word, and the Word was with God, and the Word was God. He was in the beginning with God. All things were made through Him, and without Him nothing was made that was made. In Him was life, and the life was the light of men (John 1:1–4). So if you were only born because you were made through Him—the Lord Jesus—you owe or rather borrowed your life from Him.

No matter where you were born on planet earth or who you are, you who are alive today, you were bought at a price by the redeeming Blood of Jesus Christ of Nazareth. He was sentenced to be killed for our transgressions. And even on His death row He brought a sermon, or shall I say extended His grace to those people who put Him to death on the Cross. He said, *'**Father forgive them, for they know not what they are doing.**'* (See Luke 23:34–38.)

The Lord Jesus became a Saviour to us, and a Servant to God, as it says in Isaiah 49:5–7: *"And now the Lord says, who formed Me* (**Jesus**) *from the womb to be His Servant, to bring Jacob* (it means all believers now not just the Israelites) *back to Him* (**God**) *so that Israel is gathered to Him (for I shall be glorious in the eyes of the Lord, and My God shall be My strength), indeed He says, 'It is too small a thing that You should be My Servant to raise up the tribes of Jacob, and to restore the preserved ones of Israel; I will also give You as a light to the Gentiles,* **that You should be My salvation to the ends of the earth.**'"

Thus says the Lord, the Redeemer of Israel, their Holy One, to Him whom man despises, to Him whom the nation abhors, to the Servant of rulers: "Kings shall see and arise, princes also shall worship, because of the Lord who is faithful, the Holy One of Israel; and He has chosen You." The Father chose His Only

Son.

When the Lord Jesus started His ministry, as a Servant of God and as a Messiah to the world, He chose twelve disciples as His followers and as servants to the rest of the world. He taught them using parables; He performed healing for the blind, the lame, the deaf and the mute. He also showed them how to raise the dead, and commanded the evil spirits to come out from the possessed.

After His resurrection He stayed with them for another forty days, and **instructed them to wait for the Holy Spirit**, as the comforter and the purifier of their spirit, and through that they experienced the baptism of the Holy Spirit. The Holy Spirit who guided them enabled them to speak in different kinds of tongues or languages, so that people around them were astonished at what had happened to Jesus' disciples after He ascended to heaven. And **Jesus told them that He will come back again**.

His purpose is to bring all people, not just the Jewish but also the Gentiles, closer to God. And Jacob, one of the Patriarchs of the direct lineage of Jesus, brought us to believe Jesus is the Messiah sent by God to earth to rescue us from sin. **We were all dead—spiritually unresponsive to God**—but God brought us closer through Jesus' death, using His chosen people, the Jews, to be the witnesses for us, to the end of the age; and I for one am convinced that Jesus died on the cross for me, that I may be saved from the coming judgement on the earth. *"All flesh shall know that I, the Lord, am your Saviour, and your Redeemer, the Mighty One of Jacob"* (Isaiah 49:26).

We have only One Saviour, Jesus Christ, who is the same yesterday today and forever, see Hebrews 13:8. He is the Author and Perfecter of our faith. He is the only One that can go back and erase our sins. **His whole purpose for us is to get to know Him**.

Why were you born? What was written in the Lord's book of life for you to fulfil here on earth? You were born unique; you alone can do what God has intended you to do here on earth. You have a specific role, and a specific purpose; that's why you were born. Did you choose to be born? Yes you did! Otherwise you would not be here on earth. You were either miscarried or did not exist. You wouldn't hear God's call if you didn't wish to be born. (Your ears weren't formed yet.) So His purpose for you is to step into the specific role He listed for you to do in the Book of Life, before you were even born. In Psalm 58:3 it says: *"The wicked are estranged from the womb, these who speaks lies go astray from birth."*

In Ephesians 2:10 it says: *"For we are God's handiwork created in Christ Jesus to do good works, which* **God prepared in advance for us to do.** *"* So rejoice because you've got specific things to do here on earth. And be happy that *your names are written in the book of heaven*, see Luke 10:20. It also says in Psalm 37:23: *The steps of a good man are ordered by the Lord.*

And if you do not know God personally you are invited through others who know Him now, and are now enjoying a personal relationship with the Lord Jesus. But you need to hear Him. "How could I hear God?" you may ask. Then read the Bible, that is His Word. Call Him, then listen for Him; for He said when you call He will answer. (See Jeremiah 33:3.)

Because I know Jesus loves you, He wants to have a relationship with you; and it's not a relationship of getting something from you, but actually a relationship that is giving you all the good things He wants you to have.

We are saved by God's grace through the Lord Jesus' sacrifice. Knowing this fact, you can tell the devil to back off you, so then he could not accuse you and claim your spirit and soul as his own, when you unintentionally obeyed him while you are on earth. Hold your thoughts on that…. The devil will have a license to claim your soul with him in hell even if you are unmindful of him; he will inflict you with his lies; his deceptive voice doesn't sound scary. **The only cut-off from the enemy is to accept the Lord Jesus as your Saviour**, for the devil cannot accuse Jesus of anything false before God. **When you claim His blood that washes you from all your sins, then you will be separated from the grip of the devil**. Since you accept a Holy Saviour, you make yourself holy through Him, the Saviour of your spirit and soul, so you can rely on Him to save you. He's more willing to have you as His son or as His daughter more than you will ever know!

And here is what The Lord Jesus said: *"Therefore whoever confesses Me before men, him I will also confess before My*

Father who is in heaven. But whoever denies Me before men, him I will also deny before My Father who is in heaven (Matthew 10:32–33). Also, in 1 John 2:22: *Who is a liar but he who denies that Jesus is the Christ? He is antichrist who denies the Father and the Son. Whoever denies the Son does not have the Father either; he who acknowledges the Son has the Father also.* It also says, *Jesus cannot deny Himself*; see 2 Timothy 2:13. We belong to Him, we are His—we are alive through Him, so He cannot deny us as His own. We are part of His creation, we are part of Him; that's why He made a way for us, but if you disown Him, He will disown you, before God in heaven.

How does that sound to you? Is it fair in human terms? Yes, but because He loves you and because He knows you need Him, denying you is not His purpose. And you need to claim Him as your Lord and Saviour, so that He can claim you as His child before God. Fair do's?

At the time of the flood, Noah must have warned the people that God was going to destroy all mankind because of their wickedness. (We are now in this stage of life where all sorts of wickedness abounds.) Only Noah's family, eight people in all, escaped the flood because Noah found favour in the eyes of the Lord. Noah was a righteous man, blameless among the people of his time, and he walked faithfully with God. Why am I saying this? Noah was the preacher of righteousness in his time, but his generation did not listen to him. Because before Jesus came the people were warned. After Jesus' resurrection the people of the flood heard Him preach to them. In 1 Peter 3:18–22 it says: *For Christ also suffered once for sins, the righteous for the unrighteous,* **to bring you to God.** *He was put to death in the body but made alive in the Spirit.* **After being made alive, He went and made proclamation to the imprisoned spirits—to those who were disobedient long ago when God waited patiently in the days of Noah while the ark was being built.** *In it only a few people, eight in all, were saved through water, and this water symbolizes baptism that now saves you also—not the removal of dirt from the body* **but the pledge of a clear conscience toward God.** *It saves you by the resurrection of Jesus Christ, who has gone into heaven and is at God's right hand—with angels, authorities and powers in submission to Him.*

Noah, by means of the Holy Spirit, preached the need for repentance to those who disobeyed God while the Ark was being built—and it took Noah 100 years to build the Ark. No wonder why it took so long to build it—I believe Noah was not just building but preaching to those people in his generation. (See 2 Peter 2:5.) But only seven of them believed Noah, the others refused to believe him—because they had never heard of rain before the flood; and they thought Noah was out of his mind. And **comparing to this generation, a lot of people think that when Christians speak about God and salvation we are out of our minds too**—because it doesn't taste savoury to listen to the words of righteous living. In 2 Peter 3:3–10 it says: *Scoffers will come in the last days, walking according to their own lusts, and saying, "Where is the promise of His coming? For since the fathers fell asleep, all things continue as they were from the beginning of creation." For this they wilfully forget: that by the word of God the heavens were of old, and the earth standing out of water and in the water, by which* **the world that then existed perished, being flooded with water**. *But the heavens and the earth which are now preserved by the same word are* **reserved for fire until the day of judgment and perdition of ungodly men**.

But, beloved, do not forget this one thing, that with the Lord one day is as a thousand years, and a thousand years as one day. The Lord is not slack concerning His promise, as some count slackness, but is longsuffering toward us, not willing that any should perish but that all should come to repentance.

So do not rebel against God.

Whoever you are, and whatever religion you are practising or not practising, you are known by God and you are loved by Him. For it says in Isaiah 46:9: *I am God, and there is no other; I am God, and there is none like Me. I Am the Alpha and the Omega, the beginning and the end.* (See Revelation 1: 8 and 22:13.)

You might say, "But I don't know God and how could He know me?" You may be saying to yourself, "Surely He wouldn't want to know me, because of etc., etc.," but whatever is the reason you're thinking right now, He knows it all. He knows your weaknesses, He knows your downfall, He even knows when you're sinning, and He knows your strength. And this is the truth: He saw the worst of you (and me), and He was not put off with all that He knew about you. He is still lovingly and expectantly asking you to **come and enter into His rest**.

The reason I am writing this is to let you know that there is only one true God in heaven that died for you and who loves you more than you have ever known. *No greater love is this that God gave His Only begotten Son to die on the Cross for you.* (See John 15:13 and John 3:16—paraphrased.)

And why did He do that? Because He loves His creation; we are made in His image, and every time the Lord looks down on earth and sees the hearts of people who now believe in Him, He remembers the covenant He made with Abraham, Isaac, and Jacob. These three people who obeyed His words and stood for the message of God in the first place, knew judgement was coming. So before judgement comes, ask for His compassion to fall on you, and you respond to His call; Jesus doesn't want you to be in hell.

I know right now He is knocking at the door of your heart, don't you perceive Him? He is that still small voice inside your heart. The Lord Jesus speaking in this passage said: *"Behold I stand at the door and knock. If anyone hears My voice and opens the door **I will come to him and dine with him and he with Me"*** (Rev.3:20). I tell you the truth; He is truly longing to know you and wants to have a personal relationship with you. He is looking at your heart right now and that's where you will find Him too.

Have you ever asked yourself a question like, "What is life all about? Why don't I feel complete?" Or you may be feeling there is something missing in your life; and you cannot quite put your finger on it. Have you ever wondered and asked yourself, "What is it in my life that I have? I have all these material things that I wanted and I have hankered for, for a long time, and now I feel I have achieved almost everything I wanted to achieve and I don't feel satisfied or happy or have peace in my life."

I believe from time to time we ask ourselves a question, whether we know the answer or not. I believe it's the absence or denial of the existence of God's Spirit that makes a person feel empty and void inside. Only the Spirit of God can fill that void.

Knowing that Christ, having been raised from the dead, dies no more. Death has no longer any dominion over Him. (See

Romans 6:9.) *Our life is hidden in Him when we believe, for you died, and your life is hidden with Christ in God* (Colossians 3:3). What needs to die in you this time is your will, just like Mary when she dethroned her own will, and accepted God's will in her life. You might be saying to yourself, "But I want this, and I want that," but if you already achieved it what else do you want to get hold of? How does it look like to you, your own life? Are you really happy, cosy, satisfied, and at peace? If not then my prayer for you all is: Father God, Lord Jesus and precious God the Holy Spirit, touch their hearts, and minds and give them peace, Your peace, Holy Spirit, that surpasses human understanding, and *Sanctify them,* O Lord, *by Your truth. Your word is truth* (John 17:17).

You know, when the Lord invites you, you do not need to bring presents with you to share in this occasion. All you need to bring is yourself, or maybe your broken heart so He could mend it for you.

God owns everything in heaven and on earth. What can you bring Him, but your honest heart? That's all He is asking you for.

11

IT'S VERY, VERY RUDE TO DECLINE THE LORD'S INVITATION

When someone is very kind and very good to you, you cannot help but be good back to him or her. But the Lord Jesus gave you everything you ever needed in life and what's more He is inviting you to be with Him in heaven. So truly, it's very, very rude to decline His invitation, to avoid His company in heaven together with other Christian believers, isn't it? A simple way of saying sorry to Him will enable you to receive eternal life.

And as I have already told you He's preparing a mansion, a resting place for your soul; so that you can be with Him after this frail life on earth has ended. He is calling you to be with Him forever. It's like He's wooing you, and lovingly instigating that you may know Him from your heart. **Your heart is the place where you can invite Him back.** You know, when someone has invited you, you have to invite him or her back—it's rude if you don't. And He's so longing to hear you say, "Come into my heart, be my Lord and Saviour. I … I want you to hold me in Your loving Arms; let me feel Your presence." Say to Him, "Lord, let me see You, let me taste Your goodness in the land of the living." He is a safe place for you to stay, but you have to agree with His words.

When God is about, there is true presence that surrounds people. Believe me, when you have accepted Him, it's like having a close, kind and loving friend who is invisible; but you can communicate with Him and He with you, and He knows your thoughts, but wouldn't judge you—but correct or maybe reproof you only for your own good.

You know, when a person cannot be corrected anymore, they make themselves God already, and I know there's only One true God. Everyone must bow down to Him; if you cannot bow down to God, who gave life to you and all that you have, then you have just 'high fived' the devil and welcomed him as your sphere of influence.

When God pulls back His extended hand and withdraws from you, you will come to a place of torment and no hope! That's why He wants you to have a personal relationship with Him. Wouldn't it be good to find rest and peace for your soul? In John 14:27 it says: *Peace I leave with you; my peace I give you. I do not give to you as the world gives. Do not let your hearts be troubled and do not be afraid.* And in John 15:9: ***As the Father loved Me, I also have loved you; abide in My love*** (a command).

Another invitation in Isaiah 55: 1–3: *"Come, all you who are thirsty, come to the waters; and you who have no money, come, buy and eat! Come, buy wine and milk without money and without cost. Why spend money on what is not bread, and your labour on what does not satisfy? Listen, listen to Me, and eat what is good, and you will delight in the richest of fare. Give ear and come to Me; listen, that you may live. I will make an everlasting covenant with you ...."*

You know, salvation wouldn't cost you your mortgage, your house, or your life savings. It may cost you a bit of your will, though you still have freedom. God never withdraws His freewill He gave you, so you and the Lord need to communicate. He is so, so loving and so, so good as a Father, and as Lord and Saviour. **The Lord Jesus will never ever crush your spirit and your soul**, and He will always be close to a person with a broken heart.

When someone hurts you, and says lots of hurtful words to you that you know are not true, then and there you can ask the Lord to take away your pain, overshadow your emotions, and heal the open wounds in your soul and He will do that. When someone oppresses you and accuses you of anything you know is not true, you can take your case to Him, because He can see your heart. And when you talk to Him, you will fully know He is on your side.

That's why when He was on the Cross oppressed and humiliated, He opened not His mouth. He did not bring any charges against them, but took His case to The Father, our God. He took the experience in His heart, so that when you humble yourself before Him in humility and honour, by not accusing the guilty party, but by bringing your case to Him in submission to His will, He will release and help you.

IT'S VERY, VERY RUDE TO DECLINE THE LORD'S INVITATION

You might say, "How could I, a mere man, have a relationship with the Almighty God; what kind of invitation is that?" He just said, "Come to Me." You might say, "I can't see You, I don't know where You are; how can I come?" In fact, He is so close to you (and you can come to Him in the privacy of your own bedroom) that when you still your mind or just close your eyes (to cut off the world around you) and call on Him, "Lord help me to know where You are, and to see You," He will show Himself real to you. I did so when I was a new believer.

I called and He answered; I said to Him, "Lord Jesus, Father God, I just want to see You. It's not that I don't believe You, I just want to see You." And a few days later when I stopped asking He appeared to me. I was even surprised and said in my heart, or shall I say whispered, when I saw the Lord, "What is this all about?" And the Lord said to me, "**You wanted to see Me, but don't tell anyone.**" I said, "Oh; yes," and there He was.

So come as you are. You might say to yourself, "How could I come to a God who is pure and good and holy?" But He is inviting you to *Come unto Him*. You do not need to clean yourself before you come; He's asking you to come as you are because His own blood has the cleansing power to make you pure and holy before Him. So all you have to do is to welcome Him in your heart.

Are you suffering from anxiety, illness, a broken home, or a broken relationship? He has got the answer for your problems or anything else that you may be facing right now. Are you suffering from losing someone you loved? **The Holy Spirit is the Comforter and lives in the hearts of those who have invited Him**. So if you are thinking you've got to be good before you could invite Him into your heart, you are mistaken. You cannot achieve perfection, so just come, come as you are and invite Him into your heart. He's waiting ... He's waiting ... don't ignore Him.

Why do you think He is inviting you? Because this invitation is really for every person who doesn't know the Lord Jesus yet. Let me tell you of what the Lord spoke through the prophets of long ago.

This is what He revealed to Isaiah, one of God's prophets: *"This is what the Lord says—Your Redeemer, who formed you in the womb: I am the Lord, the Maker of all things, who stretches out the heavens, who spreads out the earth by Myself"* (Isaiah 44:24). And in Isaiah 45:5–9: *"I Am the Lord, and there is no other; apart from Me there is no God. I will strengthen you, though you have not acknowledged Me, so that from the rising of the sun to the place of its setting people may know there is none besides Me. I am the Lord, and there is no other. I form the light and create darkness, I bring prosperity and create disaster; I, the Lord, do all these things.*

"You heavens above, rain down My righteousness; let the clouds shower it down. Let the earth open wide, let salvation spring up let righteousness flourish with it; I, the Lord, have created it."

Isaiah 45:18–25: *For this is what the Lord says—He who created the heavens, He is God; He who fashioned and made the earth, He founded it;* **He did not create it to be empty**, *but formed it to be inhabited—He says: "I am the Lord, and there is no other. I have not spoken in secret, from somewhere in a land of darkness; I, the Lord, speak the truth; I declare what is right. "Gather together and come; assemble, you fugitives from the nations.* **Ignorant are those who carry about idols of wood, who pray to gods that cannot save.** *Declare what is to be, present it— let them take counsel together. Who foretold this long ago, who declared it from the distant past?* **Was it not I, the Lord?** *And there is no God apart from Me, a righteous God and a Saviour; there is none but Me.*

"Turn to Me and be saved, all you ends of the earth; *for I am God, and there is no other. By myself I have sworn,* **My mouth has uttered in all integrity a word that will not be revoked**. *Before Me every knee will bow; by Me every tongue will swear. They will say of Me, 'In the Lord alone are deliverance and strength.' All who have raged against Him will come to Him and be put to shame. But all the descendants of Israel will find deliverance in the Lord and will make their boast in Him."*

If you come to Jesus Christ of Nazareth it simply means you accept Him as your Lord, Saviour and protector of your life; then you have accepted His invitation. And for those people that have accepted the Lord already but have turned back to their old ways,

IT'S VERY, VERY RUDE TO DECLINE THE LORD'S INVITATION

and forgotten God's ways, like the prodigal children of God, or have made things become idols for themselves, like drugs, money, fame, the Lord is asking you to return. Return to Him for He abundantly pardons everyone who comes to Him. His loving arms are open wide to receive you back to Him.

The enemy might make you feel guilty and ashamed, but when you ask the Lord Jesus, He always forgives—I know, He told me. So ask for His forgiveness. The longer you stay away from Him, the longer you're making your heart hardened.

In the book of Jonah the people of Nineveh were greatly sinning and the Lord had already pronounced judgement on them; but when Jonah eventually obeyed God and preached to the Ninevites, they repented wholeheartedly and put on sackcloth and fasted, animals included. Then the Lord God withdrew from sending the calamity He threatened to send, because they changed their heart's attitude towards God and God pardoned them.

Sometimes it's hard to think further ahead, knowing that we could hardly pay the mortgage for the house we are living in, or not even able to afford to climb the ladder to own our accommodation, but it is wise to think of the future of our soul, because all will die one day and everyone's spirit needs to be renewed in Christ the Lord.

This invitation comes from the heart of God that you should know Him. As the previous passages say, He knows you. Now He is giving you information. He said in John 14:6, Jesus speaking, *"I am the way, the truth, and the life. No one comes to the Father except through Me."* But isn't it true that it's very rude to refuse or decline someone's invitation flat out, without asking any question concerning the occasion? This occasion relates to your relationship with God (who gave you life), that He may protect you when you allow Him to have a say in your life. This is your assurance, that when you leave this earth you can claim your inheritance of knowing the Lord Jesus.

We know what it says in John 3:16: *For God so loved the world, that He gave His Only Son, that whoever believes in Him should not perish but have eternal life.* But in verse 18 it says: ***but whoever does not believe is condemned already**, because he has not believed in the name of the only Son of God*—**whom**

God sent on earth to redeem all people on earth.

The only truth I know is He is reliable, and the Word that came out from the mouth of our Lord Jesus came from the Living God. I know there are plenty of people who will refuse to know or be known by God, but if you are wise enough you will make that decision of knowing Him, who has the power over your spirit and soul. So make it a priority in your life now.

The Lord Jesus speaking here: *No-one can come to Me unless the Father who sent Me draws him; and* (this is the promise) *I will raise him up at the last day* (John 6:44). The truth is, no matter how much I irritate you about God's love for you, if God didn't draw you to Jesus, you cannot come anyway; but if He keeps on drawing you close to Him, don't despair, be happy—He's calling you.

The Lord Jesus is coming back for the second time on earth, **not to show His love and compassion for the whole world all over again, but to judge the whole world this time**. For He has shown His love already the first time He came to earth. He took off from Himself all the authority He had in heaven, when He was with His own Father—our God—and humbly came to submit to Father God's will. When He was on earth He was fully man, but He knew no sin and He knew He would die on the Cross for the sins of the whole world.

Did you know that **the only occasion where there is no invitation given is the funeral**? You get informed by the family of the dead who expects you to attend so you have a chance to say your last goodbye, even if you only knew that person for a short while. People will come if they valued the dead person, or even if only for the sake of the living relatives. You are informed but not normally invited.

But the Lord Jesus has a personal invitation for you, and His invitation is not burdensome. In fact His life, His death and His resurrection became the ultimate reason for this invitation He is extending to you! The Lord Jesus wants you to be with Him, not with the devil in the fiery lake of fire, where you will be forever in the **process of continual dying and decaying—but never completely dead**. So really today, if you don't know the Lord Jesus personally I am informing you.

You might say, "I'm not a fan of becoming a Christian,

IT'S VERY, VERY RUDE TO DECLINE THE LORD'S INVITATION

Christianity is not for me." But it's not a fan club. You might even joke about that you do not wish to support Jesus and His followers. You might even teasingly say, "Why do I want to know about rotting in hell?" **Because one day we will all die, you included.** As I say, "**Death is the final destination of all the living!**" You might even say, "Why would I support your theory?" Well, it's not a theory, it's a fact! Not a joke! As it says in Matthew 16:26: *What good will it be for someone to gain the whole world, yet forfeit their soul? Or what can anyone give in exchange for their soul?* The only thing I know is to believe and accept God's Testimony about His own Son's life, death and resurrection!

Right now, if you are a believer in Christ He's preparing a place for you to be with Him forever. I also want to let you know now, **there is not a single atheist in heaven who denied that God exists**; not even at its gates. God is immortal and no mortal can see Him unless He allows you to do so.

Here on earth you can get insurance for your life, so that when you die your loved ones do not have to face the uncertainty of who is going to carry the cost of your funeral expenses. You care so much for your body which will rot and go back to ashes, so while you still have time, ensure that your spirit and soul will be at peace with the Lord God in heaven and not in torment, at the lake of fire that is only intended for the devil, God's enemy. So go on and make friends with your Maker, the God of all heavens and earth.

The only humans that will be in the torment of everlasting fire are those who kept on refusing the Salvation the Lord Jesus is offering them, while alive on earth. When you sin, and there is no one on earth alive that never sins, if you ask the Lord for forgiveness, He will erase your sins—every single one of them. *For all have sinned and fall short of the glory of God—* that is Romans 3:23. And in Ecclesiastes 7:20: *There is no one on earth who is righteous, no one who does what is right and never sins.* So according to God's Word **everyone is a sinner and needs a Saviour.**

So before you decline the Lord Jesus' invitation to live in His mansion in heaven, think more than twice before you refuse it. And **make sure you invite Jesus back into your heart** to stay with you forever by the power of the Holy Spirit. You might only be renting or living in a council house or even living on the street, or maybe you own a big palatial home on earth, but at the end of your life here you cannot take anything to heaven. All your possessions will rot on earth.

Did you know that the streets in heaven are paved with pure gold? And the gates are made of pearls and all kinds of different stones, and there is crystal clear water underneath the throne of God—see Revelation 21:18–21 and Revelation 22:1. You'll miss it if you don't believe the Word of God. We all want to see that, don't we? If you can get insured on earth when one day you're here and the next day you're not, please, please, please, I beg you, insure your soul and your spirit to be with the Lord Jesus and God the Father in heaven; so you wouldn't be in the place of continuous burning in sulphur and brimstone forever.

I have a question to ask you: **If you died today, do you have assurance that you will go to heaven**? So think, if you were to die today (life is short) and if you're not sure that you are going to heaven then this is the right time to accept the Lord Jesus' invitation to receive you into His eternal dwelling; He has a mansion waiting for you up there in heaven. And you will have the assurance that you will not go to the place of unending torment.

I pray a blessing to you that you will do this and experience God's love and peace; amen and amen. Thank You Lord Jesus.

When you know that it's only God that gave life to you, and He rescued you already from the enemy's trap, then He's offering you eternal life, and preparing a mansion for to stay in heaven. Because He knows this first heaven and earth will pass away, and He has invited you to believe, that's all you can do. And if you are still in doubt, all you need to do is to ask Him to help you believe.

So truly, it's very, very rude to decline the Lord Jesus' invitation, because He is inviting you to be with Him in heaven.

12

BE READY FOR THE DAY OF THE LORD

The day of the Lord Jesus' returning on earth would bring wreckage and not peace. It would come as devastation, but before the day of the Lord comes, ungodly people will rise in power. The authorities would side on the people with repulsive teachings and unheard-of things against God. And as you can see on the news, other nations are rising up against one another. These wars and rumours of wars mentioned in the Bible have already taken place. Famines and all sorts of natural disasters which were predicted, or shall I say written in the scrolls for us to know, are happening now.

In this passage from 2 Peter 3:1–18, written thousands of years ago, and still as relevant today as it was in the Apostles' time, Peter, one of the Lord Jesus' apostles, writes:

Dear friends, this is now the second of two letters I am writing to you, in which I have been trying to stimulate your pure minds by reminding you to recall the words spoken in the past by the holy prophets and the commandment of our Lord and Saviour spoken through your apostles.

First of all you must understand this: **In the last days mockers will come and, following their own desires, will ridicule us** *by saying, "What happened to the Messiah's promise to return? Ever since our ancestors died, everything continues as it did from the beginning of creation." But they deliberately ignore the fact that long ago the heavens existed and the earth was formed by God's word out of water and with water, by which the world at that time was deluged with water and destroyed.* **Now** *by that same word,* **the present heavens and earth have been reserved for fire and are being kept for the day when ungodly people will be judged and destroyed.**

Don't forget this fact, dear friends: With the Lord a single day is like a thousand years, and a thousand years are like a single day. The Lord is not slow about his promise, as some people understand slowness, but is being patient with you. He *does not want anyone to perish, but **everyone to find room for repentance**. But the Day of the Lord will come like a thief. On that day **the heavens will disappear with a roaring sound, the elements will be destroyed by fire**, and the earth and everything done on it will be exposed.*

*Since everything will be destroyed in this way, think of the kind of holy and godly people you ought to be as you look forward to and hasten the coming of **the day of God, when the heavens will be set ablaze and dissolved and the elements will melt with fire**. But in keeping with his promise, we are looking forward to **new heavens and a new earth, where righteousness dwells**.*

So then, dear friends, since you are looking forward to this, make every effort to have the Lord find you at peace and without spot or fault. Think of our Lord's patience as facilitating salvation, just as our dear brother Paul also wrote to you according to the wisdom given him. He speaks about this subject in all his letters. Some things in them are hard to understand, which ignorant and unstable people distort, leading to their own destruction, as they do the rest of the Scriptures.

And so, dear friends, since you already know these things, continuously be on your guard not to be carried away by the deception of lawless people. Otherwise, you may fall from your secure position. Instead, continue to grow in the grace and knowledge of our Lord and Saviour Jesus, the Messiah. Glory belongs to Him both now and on that eternal day! Amen.

And in 2 Peter 1:10–21: *So then, my brothers, be all the more eager to make your calling and election certain, for if you keep on doing this you will never fail. For in this way **you will be generously granted entry into the eternal kingdom of our Lord and Saviour Jesus, the Messiah**.*

Therefore, I intend to keep on reminding you about these things, even though you already know them and are firmly established in the truth that you now have. Yet I think it is right to refresh your memory as long as I am living in this bodily tent, because I know that the removal of my bodily tent will come soon, as indeed our Lord Jesus, the Messiah, has shown me. And I will make every effort to see that you will always remember these things after I am gone.

BE READY FOR THE DAY OF THE LORD

When we told you about the power and coming of our Lord Jesus, the Messiah, we did not follow any clever myths. Rather, we were eyewitnesses of his majesty. For He received honour and glory from God the Father when these words from the Majestic Glory were spoken about Him: "This is My Son, whom I love. I am pleased with Him." **We ourselves heard this voice that came from heaven when we were with Him on the holy mountain.** *Therefore we regard the message of the prophets as confirmed beyond doubt, and you will do well to pay attention to it, as to a lamp that is shining in a gloomy place, until the day dawns and the morning star rises in your hearts. First of all, you must understand this: No prophecy in Scripture is a matter of one's own interpretation, because* **no prophecy ever originated through a human decision.** *Instead,* **men spoke from God as they were carried along by the Holy Spirit.**

You know, all appliances when bought brand new come with an instruction manual, don't they? Well, let me tell you the good news: **God came up with a manual for us—the Bible**! Our manual, the Bible, is full of instructions on how to live, as well as preparing us for life after death. And it's **not just a manual; it is fully loaded with experiences of those people long dead in the flesh, but alive in the spirit**. And as I said, we are alive because the Lord breathed on us the breath of life, our spirit; we became living souls, because we were sealed with the Spirit of the Living God.

When we read God's Word, it gives nutrients and sustenance to our soul and spirit. It lightens the burden in our minds and hearts when we experience the Holy Spirit's life-giving substance in our inner being. The experiences of the people who lived in the past, being known by God, and also those who did not know God, and those who did not have a true relationship with God, are all listed as our guide.

You might say, "How could you say that?" Let me give you an example with the story of Saul, the first King of Israel, and Samuel, the prophet of God. 1 Samuel 28:3–19: *Now Samuel was dead, and all Israel had mourned for him and buried him in his own town of Ramah. Saul had expelled the mediums and Spiritists from the land.* (Saul sort of obeyed God but half-heartedly.)

The Philistines assembled and came and set up camp at Shunem, while Saul gathered all Israel and set up camp at Gilboa. When Saul saw the Philistine army, he was afraid; terror filled his heart. He inquired of the Lord, **but the Lord did not answer** *him by dreams or Urim or prophets. Saul then said to his attendants, "Find me a woman who is a medium, so I may go and inquire of her."*

"There is one in Endor," they said.

So Saul disguised himself, putting on other clothes and at night he and two men went to the woman. "Consult a spirit for me," he said, "and bring up for me the one I name."

But the woman said to him, "Surely you know what Saul has done. He has cut off the mediums and spiritists from the land. Why have you set a trap for my life to bring about my death?"

Saul swore to her by the Lord, "As surely as the Lord lives, you will not be punished for this."

Then the woman asked, "Whom shall I bring up for you?"

"Bring up Samuel," he said.

When the woman saw Samuel, she cried out at the top of her voice and said to Saul, "Why have you deceived me? You are Saul!"

The king said to her, "Don't be afraid. What do you see?"

The woman said, "I see a ghostly figure coming up out of the earth."

"What does he look like?" he asked.

"An old man wearing a robe is coming up," she said.

Then Saul knew it was Samuel, and he bowed down and prostrated himself with his face to the ground.

Samuel said to Saul, **"Why have you disturbed me by bringing me up?"**

"I am in great distress," Saul said. (I hope you're getting what I mean here—Saul was speaking to the spirit of Samuel the prophet who was already dead.) *"The Philistines are fighting against me, and God has departed from me. He no longer answers me, either by prophets or by dreams. So I have called on you to tell me what to do."*

Samuel said, "Why do you consult me, now that the Lord has departed from you and become your enemy? **The Lord has done what he predicted through me** (it was predicted against Saul when Samuel was still alive). *The Lord has torn the kingdom out of your hands and given it to one of your neighbours—to David. Because you did not obey the Lord or carry out his fierce wrath against the Amalekites, the Lord has done this to you today. The Lord will deliver both Israel and you into the hands of the Philistines,* **and tomorrow you and your sons will be with me.** *The Lord will also give the army of Israel into the hands of the Philistines."*

The following day as the battle went on, Saul's two sons died and he too died on the same day, just as Samuel, the prophet, told him, the night he disturbed Samuel from the grave. Saul died because he was unfaithful to the Lord; he did not fully keep the commands or the word spoken by the Lord and even consulted a medium.

Even though Saul didn't obey God wholeheartedly, Saul's unfaithfulness did not make him disqualified from God's faithfulness because God is a faithful God, and He understands humans' fears and unfaithfulness. Though Saul feared the soldiers and was unfaithful to God, he and his sons went to be with Samuel in Paradise.

So you see, the Bible is the manual for the spiritual life of everyone, but you need to believe the Lord Jesus is the Saviour of the world. And whether you believe it or not, it will not change the fact that what He said in His Word—the Bible—stands forever. Whether you believe, or you don't believe, you accept it or not, it will not change the reality that God wants your soul to acknowledge Him and to return to Him. If not, it will return to the place the Bible calls 'hell'. So where would you choose to be after death, will it be in heaven or in hell? These are both reality, not fantasy. So choose right. Anyway, **what have you got to lose? If you choose the Lord Jesus, swallow your pride; it won't choke you.**

When the devil tried to tempt Jesus to turn the stone into bread, He replied, **"It is written:** *'Man does not live by bread alone, but by every Word that proceeds from the mouth of God.'"* When the Lord Jesus said "It is written" it means stated in the Bible. The Bible is the only Words that came from God, and the Ten Commandments were written by God Himself, on Mount Sinai. Everything was written about in the Bible for us to know what life is all about on earth before our time.

Our everyday existence depends on the Word of God. You may think, "How could this be?" Well, the Bible is full of the knowledge of the goodness of the Lord, and it's my food when I am fasting; detoxing my soul to cleanse my spirit.

All living beings have a soul and a spirit; **if you don't have a spirit, you are dead.**
The death in the physical means alive in spirit. The natural everyday functions in life stop when we die but the functions in the spirit carry on.

You might say, "I am not a Christian; I do not have the same values in life." But **do you value yourself** at all? What a sad, sad person you are, if you don't value yourself. How could you say you love others if you don't love yourself?

Perhaps we Christians are focused on the life eternal or the life after death, as we Christians call it. But we also focus on our life here on earth, and we practice what we believe through reading God's word, our manual, the Bible.

You may ask, what basis is there that the spirit of man is outside the body. Look around you. When someone you know dies, can they speak, can they move? Do you think they can still think? You know when the body is dead the physical brain is dead too, right? So it means the thinking is outside the head or body; right? And that thinking outside of the body is the soul and spirit of a person. What you read in the earlier passages about Saul and Samuel speaks volumes in life. This was written for us, so we know what will happen after we die. If the mediums could speak to the dead, then we know it's true today that the dead speak through the spiritualists and mediums. Although let me tell you, we shouldn't really call up any dead people, for it is said in Isaiah 8:19–20: *When someone tells you to consult mediums and spiritists, who whisper and mutter,* **should not a people enquire of their God?** *Why consult the dead on behalf of the living?* **Consult God's instruction and the testimony of warning.** *If anyone does not speak according to this word, they have no light of dawn.*

Brothers and sisters, we do not want you to be uninformed about those who sleep in death, **so that you do not grieve like the rest of mankind, who have no hope.** *Since we believe that*

Jesus died and rose again, and so we believe that **God will bring with Jesus those who have fallen asleep in Him**.

1 Thessalonians 4:13–18: *According to the Lord's word, we tell you that we who are still alive, who are left until the coming of the Lord, will certainly not precede those who have fallen asleep. For the Lord himself will come down from heaven, with a loud command, with the voice of the archangel and with the trumpet call of God, and* **the dead in Christ will rise first**. *After that,* **we who are still alive and are left will be caught up together with them in the clouds to meet the Lord in the air**. *And so we will be with the Lord for ever. Therefore* **encourage one another with these words**.

In Isaiah 46:9–10 it says: *I am God and there is no other; I Am God and there is none like Me.* **I MAKE KNOWN THE END FROM THE BEGINNING**, *from ancient times what is still to come.*

Isaiah 44:6–8: *"Thus says the Lord, the King of Israel, and His Redeemer, the Lord of hosts:* **'I Am the First and I Am the Last; besides Me there is no God. And who can proclaim as I do**? *Then let him declare it and set it in order for Me,* **since I appointed the ancient people**. *And the things that are coming and shall come, Let them show these to them. Do not fear, nor be afraid; have I not told you from that time, and declared it? You are My witnesses. Is there a God besides Me? Indeed there is no other Rock; I know not one.'"*

God enabled us to know the beginning and the end of life, or the world we are in. Old Scribes and other people like Moses wrote the first five books of the Bible. God Himself inscribed the Ten Commandments with His own Finger—see Exodus 31:18.

And in Psalm 139:14, it says: *I will praise You, for I am fearfully and wonderfully made;* **marvellous are Your works, and that my soul knows very well**.

There is a book of life, others call it the 'book of remembrance in heaven', see Revelation 3:5: *The one who is victorious will, like them, be dressed in white.* **I will never blot out the name of that person from the book of life, but will acknowledge that name before my Father and his angels**. And in Psalm 69:28: (King David's plea to God) *May they* **be blotted out of the book of life and not be listed with the righteous**.

Philippians 4:3: *Yes, and I ask you, my true companion, help these women since they have contended at my side in the cause of the gospel, along with Clement and the rest of my co-workers,* ***whose names are in the book of life*.**

Every person who was born is known by God. How true it is that there is a time to be born and a time to die. As it says in Ecclesiastes 3:1: *To everything there is a season, a time for every purpose under heaven.*

So be ready for the day of the Lord.

13

WHY DO PEOPLE BLAME GOD?

The Lord Jesus knows your beginning and your end. Sometimes we think we know our end and we think that God doesn't know anything about the world He created and about us. Allow me to inform you: **He holds our life in the palm of His merciful hand.** Some may carry on thinking, "Does God know all the calamity that's going on, here on earth? Does He even care? Does God know?" We always have questions: "How come God allowed so and so to die, if He really is a God of love? Why is there famine and all the bad events that are happening in the life of people?" But it is written that these bad events will come to the life of people, especially those who forget God, but even to those who remember God. The Bible says we will go through sufferings in life—Jesus said so, but He also said He will be with you and bring you through problems that come against you; you need only to stay with Him and take your troubles to Him in prayer. **God is not happy either that you are in this bad situation you are going through right now**; that's why He did His best to become a curse for you (and me) when he hung on the Cross and died for us. But because sin penetrated the lives of people after the fall, and since we are here on earth in our mortality, we will experience all the sufferings we know today, because life goes on that way.

And if God were to prevent every bad thing from happening, then you would think that you had no need of God. But God is always, and always will be, in control of everyone's life.

Some arrogant people may think if God is in control of their life, then they're not to be blamed for bad things they've done. Well, God intended for people to use their good common sense and not their twisted behaviour towards others. In fact, God said love your neighbour as yourself—that means you will not harm anyone because you don't want to experience harm for yourself. That is the Lord Jesus' second commandment to all people on earth; obviously not everyone is capable of loving themselves.

And if you will also just think about this: if everything always went well in life, who would call on God? Even now that you need God, you don't call on Him. How much more if you had no need of God's intervention. **If everything bad that was about to happen was prevented by Him, where would you put God in the equation of your life?** God is God and He will not give His glory to anyone. So for the sake of good, be sensible.

God made everything under heaven, and heaven above (there are three heavens as far as I know—see 2 Corinthians 12:2), and you are included as the work of His hand. You may be able to blame everybody and exclude yourself, but you know you are accountable for your own actions by the law of the land. And God gave us freewill for our benefit, not treating us as robots, who would say, "Yes, God, at Your service, God; I bow down to Your will, God."

That freewill we have is our license to react to God in love and reverence and honour towards His goodness to us all. God so loves us that He gave us freewill. God's intention for us is to have a proper relationship with Him as His people and His children, not as puppets or robots! **So no one could say, I am subservient to God's every whim against my very own will.** So He can be our God, our Saviour, our Peace, our Joy, our contentment in life. He supplies our needs to make us feel complete and contented.

The One who truly loves us is God; whom people always blame for everything. Whether you are white, brown, black, yellow, blue—whatever your colour and race—remember it's God who put your spirit in your mother's womb; you do not have a say as to which country you are going to be born in and who's parenting you. God is Sovereign; do not belittle God's power over your life; **you can never fight God and win over Him, Satan did that and he lost, and is still losing today.** And you know what? By the Power of the blood of Jesus Christ of Nazareth and His cross we have been given power to fight against the enemy's devices against us. And God gave us the Holy Spirit who lives in us (only if we have Him as our Saviour and Lord), that's why it says in 1 John 4:4: ***He who is in you, is greater than he who is in the world.***

When people become greedy for material wealth, or become

kidnappers, murderers, suicide bombers, abusers, or paedophiles, **how does that become God's fault**? So many people blame God for the wrong they see, but they never blame the devil .... If you are a true friend to someone you would never blame your true friend; you would cover up for them, wouldn't you? If you don't like someone or you are an enemy to someone you would always have bad things to say about them, and you would blame them, wouldn't you? Just think about it .... I would like to ask you, "Who is your enemy, and who is your friend? Are you now an enemy of God?"

Why do some people keep on blaming God? "Why this and why that, God?" they would ask. "Why didn't He protect my relatives or friends from being mugged or murdered or raped or killed or being abused ...?" They would say, "If Christians are right by saying God is love, where is the love in that then?" And by saying such words to God you are putting your friends and relatives higher and bigger than God, belittling God's authority; that's also the devil's way!

But God gave people freedom, and He allows them to make decisions for themselves. God didn't attach strings to us to make us like His puppets, no! He gave us freewill, and will not violate our own will. But **with this freedom we have, He wouldn't override our will, whether good or bad**. The fact is, **God as Almighty as He is, will never ever overstep the freedom of choice He has given us**.

Love covers a multitude of sins. God doesn't expose your sins, He covers them for you, but you need to talk to Him discreetly. He is not the God that exposes us, He is the God that covers. And that's why God covers you by the blood of Jesus when you believe and ask Him to lead you. Although God is very powerful, He does not violate our rights when we sin, **otherwise forgiveness would not be necessary**; He wouldn't then have needed to die on the Cross to forgive the sins of the whole world. If God killed everyone who sinned, I wouldn't be writing this book, and you would not be reading this either, if you know what I mean—it means we are both dead. *For all have sinned and fall short of the glory of God* (Romans 3:23). *There is no one righteous, no, not one* (Romans 3:10). *Surely there is not a righteous man on earth who does good and never sins*

(Ecclesiastes 7:20).

God's love does not apply only to those we think are good in the natural—like ourselves, relatives, friends and so forth and so on—as God, being all-powerful and all loving, does not have the same mind as we do. Our minds are only focused on ourselves, friends and relatives or acquaintances, but **God's mind is focused on the whole world**; that's why He died for the whole world, not just for a few people like your family and friends. He cares for everyone, yet when He is dealing with you, you feel that it's only you He loves and is dealing with, and no one else.

God's thoughts are higher than our thoughts and His ways are higher than our ways (see Isaiah 55:8–9). We are all self-centred, not always mindful of others, but God loves every single person alive today! Can you argue with God, who gives life to you? Job tried to and he didn't win. But God is gracious and even upheld Job's integrity before the enemy when God told him, *"There is not a just man on earth like Job who shuns evil"* (see Job 1:8). Everything comes from God, let me just remind you again. God told Job about creation (see Job chapters 38–40).

I see it as this: The Lord Jesus agreed in the first place for the creation of the world to take place. If the Lord Jesus hadn't agreed with Father God (but how could He refuse? He is God's Word in heaven) He could not have sent Him to earth. **The Lord Jesus is the heart of Father God who brings healing and peace to all who'd come to Him**. Remember that He said that He could only do the work He saw His Father doing.

Now I believe God tests His people: He tested King Hezekiah to see what was in his heart; and the Lord tested even King David, when he counted the fighting men in Israel. He knew that not by the number of fighting men were battles won by the Israelites, but by the help of God.

Job's integrity was also tested, as was king Nebuchadnezzar. This is what is says in the book of Daniel 4:4–35: *I, Nebuchadnezzar, was at home **in my palace, contented and prosperous*** (being in a palace wealthy and contented doesn't make you complete, you need God to complete you). *I had a dream that made me afraid. As I was lying in bed, the images and visions that passed through my mind terrified me. So I commanded that all the wise men of Babylon be brought before* me to interpret the dream for me. When the magicians, enchanters, astrologers and diviners came, I told them the dream, but they could not interpret it for me. Finally, Daniel came into my presence and I told him the dream. (He is called Belteshazzar, after the name of my god and the spirit of the holy gods is in him.)

I said, "Belteshazzar, chief of the magicians (Daniel was a prophet of God, not a magician, as Nebuchadnezzar addressed him), *I know that the spirit of the holy gods is in you, and no mystery is too difficult for you. Here is my dream; interpret it for me. These are the visions I saw while lying in bed: I looked, and there before me stood a tree in the middle of the land. Its height was enormous. The tree grew large and strong and its top touched the sky; it was visible to the ends of the earth. Its leaves were beautiful, its fruit abundant, and on it was food for all. Under it the wild animals found shelter, and the birds lived in its branches; from it every creature was fed.*

"In the visions I saw while lying in bed, I looked, and there before me was a Holy One, a messenger, coming down from heaven. He called in a loud voice: 'Cut down the tree and trim off its branches; strip off its leaves and scatter its fruit. Let the animals flee from under it and the birds from its branches. But let the stump and its roots, bound with iron and bronze, remain in the ground, in the grass of the field.

"'Let him be drenched with the dew of heaven, and let him live with the animals among the plants of the earth. **Let his mind be changed from that of a man and let him be given the mind of an animal, till seven times pass by for him.**

"'The decision is announced by messengers, the holy ones declare the verdict, so that the living may know that **the Most High is Sovereign over all kingdoms on earth** *and gives them to anyone He wishes and sets over them the lowliest of people.*

"This is the dream that I, King Nebuchadnezzar, had. Now, Belteshazzar, tell me what it means, for none of the wise men in my kingdom can interpret it for me. But you can, because the spirit of the holy gods is in you."

Then Daniel (also called Belteshazzar) was greatly perplexed for a time, and his thoughts terrified him. So the king said, "Belteshazzar, do not let the dream or its meaning alarm you."

Belteshazzar answered, "My lord, if only the dream applied to your enemies and its meaning to your adversaries! The tree you saw, which grew large and strong, with its top touching the sky, visible to the whole earth, with beautiful leaves and abundant fruit, providing food for all, giving shelter to the wild animals, and having nesting places in its branches for the birds—**Your Majesty, you are that tree!** You have become great and strong; your greatness has grown until it reaches the sky, and your dominion extends to distant parts of the earth.

"Your Majesty saw a Holy One, a messenger, coming down from heaven and saying, 'Cut down the tree and destroy it, but leave the stump, bound with iron and bronze, in the grass of the field, **while its roots remain in the ground**. Let him be drenched with the dew of heaven; let him live with the wild animals, until seven times pass by for him.'

"This is the interpretation, Your Majesty, and **this is the decree the Most High has issued against my lord the king**: You will be driven away from people and will live with the wild animals; you will eat grass like the ox and be drenched with the dew of heaven. Seven times will pass by for you **until you acknowledge that the Most High is Sovereign over all kingdoms on earth** and gives them to anyone He wishes. The command to leave the stump of the tree with its roots means that your kingdom will be restored to you when you acknowledge that Heaven rules. Therefore, Your Majesty, be pleased to accept my advice: **Renounce your sins by doing what is right, and your wickedness by being kind to the oppressed**. It may be that then your prosperity will continue."

All this happened to King Nebuchadnezzar; Twelve months later, as the king was walking on the roof of the royal palace of Babylon, he said, "Is not this the great Babylon I have built as the royal residence, by my mighty power and for the glory of my majesty?"

Even as the words were on his lips, **a voice came from heaven**, "This is what is decreed for you, King Nebuchadnezzar: Your royal authority has been taken from you. You will be driven away from people and will live with the wild animals; you will eat grass like the ox. Seven times will pass by for you until you acknowledge that the Most High is sovereign over all kingdoms *on earth and gives them to anyone He wishes."*

Immediately what had been said about Nebuchadnezzar was fulfilled. *He was driven away from people and ate grass like the ox. His body was drenched with the dew of heaven until his hair grew like the feathers of an eagle and his nails like the claws of a bird. At the end of that time,* **I, Nebuchadnezzar, raised my eyes toward heaven, and my sanity was restored. Then I praised the Most High; I honoured and glorified Him who lives forever.**

His dominion is an eternal dominion; His kingdom endures from generation to generation. All the peoples of the earth are regarded as nothing. He does as He pleases with the powers of heaven and the peoples of the earth. No one can hold back His hand or say to Him: "What have You done?"

The Lord Jesus didn't come to earth for the sinless and the healthy, and the found. **The Lord Jesus came for the sick, the sinners and the lost**—see Matthew 9:13 & Matthew 18:11. Even though you didn't do anything good or bad yet, God already loved you—past tense. And we are God's workmanship; He is continuously loving us and He wants to bring us back into a relationship with Him as it was before the fall of man. God is longing for us to come back to Him, with all our hearts. But the enemy has had a grip on humans' minds since the fall of man, when they obeyed him—unintentionally of course. We need our minds renewed.

And God wants to build a church in human hearts. The church will be the bride of Christ and Christ Himself is the Groom. As we know, in all God's chosen people, there is not one Prophet or King or anyone else worthy enough to take that step to pull us out of the enemy's grip. Jesus is the only sacrifice that will be accepted for the Father God's bride—we are that bride, the Christian believers (the church)—to take us out of the enemy's hand. We subjected ourselves continually to the devil unintentionally, because we didn't know the consequences of our actions; the same as Adam and Eve. They too didn't know the consequences of their actions before they were tested; they only knew God then.

Everything failed through humans' choice. God was so grieved in His heart that all activities under heaven were continually evil in His sight, with regard to human deeds.

There's no worthy enough dowry for the Father to take back the bride (the church). Father God could not snatch us out from the hands of the enemy, so He offered His only Son. The **Lord Jesus Christ stepped in and put Himself forward as the dowry for His bride, the church**—the people God had created.

And Father God accepted the only holy, pure, unblemished sacrifice that is our Lord Jesus Himself. God said, *"You are My beloved Son, with You I Am well pleased"* (see Mark 1:11). So the relationship between heaven and earth, and between God and man was brought together through the reconciliation of Jesus' death and sacrifice. And since all creation was made through Him and for Him, Jesus was the only One qualified to do the job. He was the only One worthy to stand before Father God, and became our dowry for God the Father, so the church and Christ will become one. And since He was with God from the beginning, He could not shrink back from the whole concept of being the dowry for the bride. He Himself was willing to suffer for our sake, and it's not for the goodness or even the benefit of God, but it's for our own benefit that we are rescued from God's enemy, our enemy.

Jesus is the only One acceptable in God's sight to become the sacrificial lamb. Being pure and spotless before God the Father, the Lord Jesus, His Son, became the sacrificial Lamb for our transgressions and our iniquities.

As all brides need a dowry, Jesus Christ Himself became that dowry. There was no other worthy enough dowry for Father God to accept; **we are too expensive for God to lose us** to the devil. **Jesus Christ paid for us the full sacrifice, and purchased our souls from the enemy's hands**. Father God had demanded to purchase every soul, and every spirit of man, for Christ. **Only Jesus' blood in the court of heaven and on earth has the power** to do what He has done for us, to remove the sin of any man or woman. Every single person alive today, and those who lived before us, fall short of the glory of God—see Romans 3:23.

The thought behind all this truth is only Jesus has the power to die for the world and He did, for the sake of God's creation. If you read Revelation 4:11 this is what it says: *"You are worthy, our Lord and God, to receive glory and honour and power,* ***for you created all things****, and* ***by your will they were created****.* And in Revelation 5:1–9: *Then I saw in the right hand of Him who sat on the throne a scroll with writing on both sides and sealed with seven seals. And I saw a mighty angel proclaiming in a loud voice, "Who is worthy to break the seals and open the scroll?"* But **no one in heaven or on earth or under the earth could open the scroll or even look inside it**. *I wept and* wept (this was John who received the Revelation and wrote the book) *because no one was found who was worthy to open the scroll or look inside. Then one of the elders said to me, "Do not weep!* **See, the Lion of the tribe of Judah, the Root of David, has triumphed. He is able to open the scroll and its seven seals."* (That was the Lord Jesus.)

Then I saw a Lamb, looking as if it had been slain, standing at the centre of the throne, encircled by the four living creatures and the elders. The Lamb had seven horns and seven eyes, which are the **seven spirits of God** *sent out into all the earth. He went and took the scroll from the right hand of Him who sat on the throne. And when He had taken it, the four living creatures and the twenty-four elders fell down before the Lamb. Each one had a harp and they were holding golden bowls full of incense, which are* **the prayers of God's people**. *And they sang a new song, saying: "You are worthy to take the scroll and to open its seals, because You were slain, and* **with Your blood You purchased for God, persons from every tribe and language and people and nation**.*"*

In Revelation 8:1 it says: *When He* (Jesus) *opened the seventh seal, there was silence in heaven for half an hour.*

Did you know that the devil was an anointed cherub, his anointing remains in him, and today he works in that anointing to trip us back into his cage or dungeon? He is the spirit in the air that mutters to the mediums and spiritualists in today's life. That is why it says in the book of Isaiah 8:19 that we shouldn't associate with these spirits in the air if they don't have the light of day—that Light which is God and the Lord Jesus combined with the Holy Spirit is the Light and life of all men (paraphrased). God forbids His people to seek psychics. This is rife today under the world's influence; a lot of people are fooled by it, as they think these are friendly spirits, because the spiritualists, mediums and psychics know how to communicate with the dead and tell them half the truth; but be warned, these are the spirits of the Anti-Christ. Because of the freedom of choice, even the Angels of God who have power and authority over us were sometimes the victims of their own selves and became anti-Christs.

Before Jesus' death, the church did not exist; only after Jesus' death did the church exist. The dowry was paid for by Jesus; He purchased us all for Father God, so that we could be brought back to the Almighty God. It is explained in 1 Corinthians 15:20–22, and this is what it says: *But now Christ is risen from the dead, and has become the firstfruits of those who have fallen asleep. For since by man came death, by Man also came the resurrection of the dead.* ***For as in Adam all die, even so in Christ all shall be made alive.*** So the Lord Jesus needed to die, for it says in John 12:24: *Very truly I tell you,* ***unless a grain of wheat falls to the ground and dies, it remains only a single seed. But if it dies, it produces many seeds.***

No one would be saved if it remained a single seed, but if it dies it would create more seeds—more seeds—more believers in Christ will be brought back to God. God has planned for you to be with Him forever, but you have to step into God's plan for you and your family line.

And why are we so very important to God? Does He really need us? No, He doesn't; but because Father God loves us, and His Son He couldn't devalue Jesus or take His sacrifice for granted. God has a good plan for us, to live alongside Him and be the children He expected us to be. So be where you can still find God's grace for you. Be also aware that God is testing human hearts to see if we will follow Him wholeheartedly, and some will do, but there will always be some who would not, because of our freewill. Make sure you're not one of those who disbelieve God's Word.

You may have heard that God will judge all people on earth. In this passage, 2 Timothy 4:1–8, Paul the apostle was writing to Timothy his son: *In the presence of God and of Christ Jesus,* ***who will judge the living and the dead****, and in view of His appearing and His kingdom, I give you this charge: preach the word; be prepared in season and out of season; correct, rebuke and encourage—with great patience and careful instruction. For* *the time will come when people will not put up with sound doctrine. Instead, to suit their own desires, they will gather round them a great number of teachers to say what their itching ears want to hear.* **They will turn their ears away from the truth and turn aside to myths.** *But you, keep your head in all situations, endure hardship, do the work of an evangelist, and discharge all the duties of your ministry.*

Now there is in store for me the crown of righteousness, which the Lord, the righteous Judge, will award to me on that day—and not only to me, but also to all who have longed for His appearing.

The Lord Jesus' second coming, whether you believe it or not, is going to happen, because the Lord Jesus said so! He will pronounce judgement on all the inhabitants of the earth. And His second coming is near; in fact it will be very, very soon, so make sure you are not included in those people who will be judged.

If you're saying to yourself, "How will I know all these things are going to happen?" Well, read the Bible, which is God's Word.

You probably have life insurance on earth, to make sure your loved ones wouldn't be burdened with your funeral expenses and so on, plus you want to leave them some of your money and the things you worked so hard for to get. That's very good, in fact, that is very, very good—yes, well done! **But don't you want to make sure that you will have assurance of everlasting life in heaven, as the resting place of your soul**?

It would be too late for you after you've breathed your last breath, for you have no power to control your spirit and your soul when you're dead. And you cannot bypass the Lord Jesus' authority over you. For this is what is says in John 14:6: *"I am Way, the Truth and the Life. No man comes to the Father except through Me."* Admit to God that you need a Saviour, because **you know there is life after death**! If you don't know yet then I am telling you now! The Lord Jesus has already provided for your salvation, and it's your right to claim it for yourself; you need His saving grace so you would be in heaven with Him.

The streets in heaven are paved with gold and there is running water under His throne—pure, clear, unadulterated water, where you can drink and never thirst again. The gates of heaven are made of precious stones. There is no need of the sun or moon as Jesus is the light that shines in there. All your relatives and friends who have accepted Jesus as their own personal Saviour and protector of their lives will be there with you.

There is a chasm that separates people, where you will see all the arrogant and condemned people who refused to believe the Lord Jesus. Those people will be there, far away from you. You cannot come across to them and they cannot come across to you and your loved ones (see Luke 16:19–31).

All you need to do is lower your pride and ask for forgiveness from the Lord Jesus (He is the only way to heaven—see John 14:6) and believe His death and resurrection, so that when you die, you can be resurrected by Him, who died for all, including you (see 2 Corinthians 5:15). So turn away from all the bad things you know are not the right things to do. Confess your sins that you may be forgiven.

In John 11:25–26: (the Lord Jesus speaking to Martha) Jesus said to her, *"I am the resurrection and the life. Whoever believes in Me, though he die, yet shall he live, and everyone who lives and believes in Me shall never die. Do you believe this?"* She spoke of the natural process of her brother's body decaying in the tomb, where he had been for four days, while the Lord Jesus spoke to her through the eyes of faith and helped Martha's unbelief. The Lord Jesus also encouraged Jairus, a synagogue leader; He told him, ***"Don't be afraid; just believe"*** (See Luke 8:50).

The Lord always helps people's unbelief. The Lord could say to the mountain, "Throw yourself in the sea and this mountain will obey the Lord Jesus' commands and do it, according to His own faith with His Father, our God.

The Lord Jesus' faith is based on His personal relationship with His own Father, our God. And we too could have that relationship with the Lord, and He will do what we ask of Him, when we believe. When we say that our faith is not based on religion, but based on our relationship with the Lord Jesus, we mean our relationship is spiritual, because God is a Spirit. This is what we believe through reading His Word, the Bible. And since Father God had already sent the promised Holy Spirit to His disciples, when we believe in Him, we too now have access to the Holy Spirit of God.

The Lord Jesus was full of the Holy Spirit because He was birthed in Him by God. But for us we need an anchor, and the Lord Jesus is our anchor in faith; for it is only through Him we could access and experience the presence and the power of the Holy Spirit.

Okay, somebody may stubbornly say, "I don't need Jesus or God. I don't need a Saviour, and about the Holy Spirit—how could you have a relationship with the invisible one, like wind?" You might even say to yourself, "Well, I didn't kill anyone; I didn't lust after any woman or man; I never, ever tell lies to anybody or withhold the truth from anyone; I never ever stole from anyone (not even my sister's or my brother's sweets); I never ever think bad about any person, or I've never, ever used foul language in my whole life, or swear badly against anybody, not even when I'm drunk, or driving?" Really? Oh, really! Well then you are a perfect person, aren't you? Well done to you, you should be in heaven now, you arrogant! Because it says in Ecclesiastes 7:20: *for there is not a just man on earth who does what is right and never sins*. Well then, where is your basis that you have never ever sinned?

If God would not hold anyone accountable for their sins, then Jesus died for nothing. If you do not denounce your sin, then Jesus could not save you. The simple answer is if you accept and believe you are a sinner, and His death and resurrection is the only hope you're holding on to—that is His grace, not human effort—then the justice and mercy of the Lord will come as your defence because you believe in the One the Father God has claimed to eradicate your sins.

If you are saying, "I cannot force myself to believe; I don't know if I have to believe that all these things about Jesus are true," then ask the Lord yourself, "Is it true, Lord Jesus, that if I didn't accept You as my Saviour or if I did not acknowledge You here on earth, You will not acknowledge me in front of God in heaven, and judge me instead when I die?" The Lord Jesus might say to you, "Son, daughter, I love you; but it would be the devil who will accuse you in front of My Father in heaven—not Me, and how could I rescue you if you don't believe in Me; who am I to you?"

It's your soul that will be judged if you don't believe the word of God—not your physical body, because that will be rotting in the ground. But your soul, which feels the pain and every emotion, will live forever, and in that, my friend, you will be judged. Not my word, but God's Original Word, for this is what it says in John 3:15–21: *That everyone who believes may have eternal life in Him." For God so loved the world that he gave His one and only Son, that whoever believes in Him shall not perish but have eternal life. For God did not send His Son into the world to condemn the world, but to save the world through Him. Whoever believes in Him is not condemned, but* **whoever does not believe stands condemned already** *because they have not believed in the name of God's one and only Son. This is the verdict: Light has come into the world, but people loved darkness instead of light because their deeds were evil. Everyone who does evil hates the light, and will not come into the light for fear that their deeds will be exposed. But whoever lives by the truth comes into the light, so that it may be seen plainly that what they have done has been done in the sight of God.*

But if you say, "Lord Jesus, forgive me, I'm a sinner, I acknowledge that You O Lord are righteous, please save my spirit and my soul from the judgement that will come to everyone living, and dead; lead me please and guide me in Your truth, in Jesus name, Amen," then you wouldn't be judged.

If you still don't believe me, and don't listen and wouldn't wish to read the Bible, then at least I have given you something to mull over. If you're saying, "Why would I listen to you, Naylee, and who are you and these other people who told me about this Jesus as your Lord over my soul, body, and spirit and how would that affect me?" In many ways it will affect your soul and spirit, because your life on earth is borrowed from God, and He will require it back, you do not have control over your spirit and soul when it leaves your body, ok? And when you do not have a relationship with the Lord Jesus, it means He will not claim your spirit man as His. And now I am telling you, because the Lord Jesus commanded us who believe in Him now, to go and tell the whole world about His personal love for you, His second coming, His death and resurrection and that heaven and hell are waiting. The Lord also said to us that we should love our neighbour as ourselves, and though you may not be my immediate neighbour, but as a fellow human being, I don't want anyone to be in hell; I'd rather prefer to know that you will be in heaven. When it's time for you to say, "Bye, bye, earth," you can say "Hello heaven." And the Lord Jesus will welcome you there. Rather than when your spirit leaves your body and you die, the enemy will greet you with, "Welcome to hell!"

Although I might not have the opportunity to speak to you personally, at least I can tell you through this book. If you're saying to yourself, "I'm an atheist and that wouldn't affect me," well, I'm telling you, it *will* truly affect you when you are in front of the throne of God and He is asking you, "Why didn't you believe those Christians who told you about the way to Me?" It might not affect your belief on earth, but it will affect your soul and spirit, so please don't be stubborn. God's word is Supreme over all. You're only the dust of the earth. Anyway, you do not have power over your soul, or spirit or even your body. **Once you are dead, you will have no control over your spirit**. What are you going to do, if you find out that you're dead and you're in hell? It would be too late for you to do anything or say anything. And then you find out that those Christians have told you the truth about the Lord Jesus and heaven, and hell. And you cannot go back or do the things you think you can do, after you die! What then?

Did you know that there are invisible thrones, and there are kingdoms that Only God knows about, and there are principalities and powers over all those kingdoms too? See Colossians 1:16. If you don't believe in God's Word and teaching, who would you believe in, the devil? You might say, "I've never seen the devil either, how would I know there is one?" Well, I'm telling you, one third of all the angels became the devil who spreads lies and wants you to believe them. There are evil spirits in heaven as well as on earth—those who followed the snake, who tempted the first human beings, became the devil. **The truth is, God's word has the supreme power over all He has made**. And the Lord Jesus Himself said, **He was not sent to condemn** the world, in the first place, but to save the world—all people on earth have sinned and will only be saved through Him. Jesus said: *For I did not come to call the righteous but sinners to repentance* (see Matthew 9:13), for no one is sinless in God's eyes.

This is the Lord Jesus' own Testimony about Himself **not condemning on His first coming,** but condemning on **His second coming. There will be eternal judgement for those who refused to believe in Him.** They are condemned already **for they are making the Lord Jesus to be a liar.** There is only one God of truth that came and went back to heaven, and He will be back again; not to carry on loving, but this time to judge.

Think about it, even the very breath in you today is from Him. You would never be on this earth if you didn't agree beforehand to come and live here on earth. For He said, "Before I formed you in the womb, I called you." So if you did not answer it means you did not hear God's call, and you did not agree to be born. Yes, He gave you freedom of choice also, but if you are wise enough you would choose Him, who owns the land, the sea, the sky and all inhabitants of the earth, for He created it all, see Jeremiah 51:15 and Psalms 24:1–3.

You might say, "I'll go to another planet." Oh, just to remind you, God owns that too. It says in John 1:1–3: *In the beginning was the Word, and the Word was with God, and the Word was God. He was with God in the beginning. Through Him all things were made; without Him nothing was made that has been made.* Does God says these things just to lie? No! In Numbers 23:19: **God is not human that He should lie**, *not a human being that He should change His mind. Does He speak and then not act? Does He promise and not fulfil?*

The majority of people who blame God are those who do not even have a personal relationship with Him. Most of them know that God has the power to protect and to stop bad events happening, but maybe they are expecting that God will come and rescue them without their making an effort to call on God! But God said, "Come to Me, call unto Me!" Did you come? Did you call? Perhaps you forget that God is an Almighty God and will never be subject to any human's threat.

God is a Gentle God, He does not push in; He does not barge into your life; He never violates humans' right of choice and freedom. No! Absolutely not! But you may find it is the nature of the enemy to impose in your life, to barge in, to accuse you, to lie to you—that is the enemy's nature. He will never give you any choice; he will always abruptly and rudely impose on what you should do and say, and holds grudges and inflicts bad attitudes and thoughts towards your fellow human beings. The exact opposite of what God says to us: *"Love your neighbour as yourself."* But God will come when you invite Him into your life.

And it says in 2 Chronicles 7:14 (God speaking here): *"If My people who are called by My name will humble themselves, and pray and seek My face, and turn from their wicked ways, then I will hear from heaven, and will forgive their sin and heal their land."* When it says: *If My people who are called by My name*— it means those who are already believing and having a relationship with Him as His children and He as our Father God. *Will humble themselves and pray and seek My face* means to humble yourself before Him, to give Him an authority and a say over your life, as He guides and leads you. And to *pray* means to ask according to His will. To *seek His face* is to enquire of Him before you do anything; put Him first. And to *turn from their wicked ways* is to make God your God in everything you do!

After you do all those things on God's terms, then God has a promise and said, *"Then I will hear from heaven, and will forgive their sin, and heal their land ...."* It means He will answer your prayers in the most positive way, and restore you to a place where He wants you to be, and prosper your soul with the blessings of peace, satisfaction, contentment and prosperity in your life. It might not be in terms of financial gain or material wealth, but it could also be that way. The Lord knows what you need before you ask, but He wants you to prove to Him that you are in need of Him.

God will not surrender to you! It's you who need to surrender to God.

14

MAKE EVERY EFFORT TO BE HEAVEN'S RESIDENT

I think it is quite a comforting thought that one day there will be an end to all the physical ailments of one's body, especially the effects of old age—when we could hardly lift a cup of tea or coffee into our mouths without spilling it, or when we have to shuffle our feet or drag our legs along to walk, and pop our dentures into our mouths and balance our glasses onto our noses, and put hearing aids into our ears, and walking sticks into our hands. Can you imagine, when you wake up in the morning, you lift your head off your pillow, and ease your old back off your bed, put your slippers on, feel for your glasses where you placed them the night before, and shuffle your way out to the toilet? It would feel like an endless task before you could even start your day. It will be such a relief when one day all the physical sufferings and hardship will end and your soul will rest peacefully in God's destined place for you, by knowing God personally.

We know we all love our own family more than we love ourselves, and as parents we need to be concerned about our children's salvation. We need to leave them in the capable Hands of God, knowing that they too will be in the same place where we will be; that, I say, will make our hearts content when they come to know the God we know!

Then I saw "a new heaven and a new earth," for the first heaven and the first earth had passed away, and there was no longer any sea. I saw the Holy City, the new Jerusalem, coming down out of heaven from God, prepared as a bride beautifully dressed for her husband. And I heard a loud voice from the throne saying, "Look! God's dwelling place is now among the people, and he will dwell with them. They will be His people, and God himself will be with them and be their God. 'He will wipe every tear from their eyes. There will be no more death' or mourning or crying or pain, for the old order of things has passed away (Revelation 21:1–4).

Life on earth is too short, but in heaven we will live for eternity, or until the Lord God Almighty restores back to earth what He first intended to happen. Then the Lord will bring down the new heaven and the new earth to Jerusalem, where there will be no more water.

The sea was the place of the devil which will never ever exist again. Exactly what will happen after, only God knows. We only get a little glimpse from what the Bible tells us.

But I have a question to ask: Do you think you're automatically going to heaven? It would be such a comforting thought if it were so. The sad thing is I know not everyone who dies will go to heaven. Even if you think, or even if everyone said to you that you are good man or woman—and yes, maybe everything you did was with good intentions—but you do not have a relationship with God, then you still have fallen short of God's glory. The only way to have a relationship with God is to believe in Jesus Christ and that he died for your sins. God will never push away anyone who comes to Him. Heaven is a place where God's love and peace reign, because God is there.

When you have the assurance that your soul and spirit will have a rest in heaven when you die, that I say is a very comforting truth. Knowing that God said, *"Heaven is My throne and the earth is My footstool"* (see Isaiah 66:1 and Acts 7:49–50), then may I say whichever part of the planet you are on, **God is ruling**.

Supposing you do not have an assurance where your spirit or soul will stay. Can you really just say, "Que sera, sera, whatever will be, will be?" Maybe here on earth yes, but what happens when you die? For those of us who have a relationship with the Lord Jesus now, when our end comes it will truly be a comforting feeling knowing that we have that assurance we will be with Him in Heaven, where there will be no more pain—physical, mental, and emotional. But for those people who refuse to acknowledge the Lord Jesus it will be a different outcome. Because the Lord Jesus said, *"Whoever believes in him* (Jesus) *is not condemned, but whoever does not believe is condemned already, because he has not believed in the name of the only Son of God.*

Everyone knows that death will come to all; whether we are rich or poor, good or bad, well known or unknown, every single person breathing air in their lungs will one day die; but our spirit man—and every living person has a soul and a spirit—will live forever.

There is a waiting place for our soul and spirit before the Lord Jesus' second coming takes place. When I was in the Roman Catholic religion (and it is a religion) I thought that when a person died he or she would go to purgatory, not to hell straightaway. But when I started reading the Bible I found out that the believers in Christ Jesus who hope for His forgiveness will actually be staying in the Paradise of God, not purgatory. I don't know where purgatory comes from, but it is not in the Bible.

The Bible records at Jesus' crucifixion there were two criminals hanging next to Him. One of them said to the Lord Jesus, *"Remember me when You come into Your Kingdom,"* and the Lord Jesus assured him and said, *"Today you will be with Me in Paradise"* (see Luke 23:42–43). That Paradise the Lord Jesus was talking about is where the tree of life was, which was guarded by the cherubim after Adam and Eve sinned, before the Lord God threw them out of the Garden of Eden. See Genesis 3:22–24 and Revelation 2:7.

Are you afraid of dying? Some people, even those who call themselves Christians, are afraid that their spirit when it leaves their body will go to the other world where God is not present, or it will not meet with God. But when you make the decision that the Lord Jesus is your Saviour, you can rest assured that your destination is God's kingdom. The Holy Spirit will guide you and if you are still unsure, let me just tell you this: **God's relationship with you is real**.

If you are still scared, then do this: Place your hand on your heart, ask the Holy Spirit to take away your fear and give you peace, and let the Holy Spirit rest in your heart. If you are holding any grudges or heartfelt pain for other people's unkind actions or words towards you, then release them, by simply saying to the Lord Jesus, "I forgive them, I release them, Father God, and bless them with every blessing they need this time and release me, Father, from them. May Your peace lead me, O

God—lead me to know, really, really know You." God will accept you since you have invited Him into your heart.

For those who carry on refusing to believe the Lord Jesus' word, there is no assurance where their spirit will go after they die, but for everyone who believes in Jesus' death and resurrection, they will know where their spirit will go. Jesus said in Psalm 31:5 when He was hanging on the Cross: *"Father into Your hands I commit My Spirit."* The fact that the Lord Jesus had committed His own Spirit to His Father, our God (His very own Dad), before His spirit Man departed from His body, is an eye opener. Knowing this, we must commit our own spirit to Jesus, the only way to God.

God the Father gave Him all the power and authority that was His before He came down from heaven to earth before He became Jesus our Lord, and Saviour and protector of our lives. He was 'The Word' in heaven with God; and He was with God at the time of Creation, see John 1:3.

God left everything to the Lord Jesus' hand. All judgement belongs to Him now, see Romans 3:23–26. It says: (we are) *being **justified freely by His grace through the redemption that is in Christ Jesus**.* In John 5:30 it says: *I can of Myself do nothing. As I hear, I judge; and My judgement is righteous, because I do not seek My own will but the will of the Father who sent Me.* Also, in Ecclesiastes 12:7 it says: *And* **the spirit (of man)** *will return to God who gave it.*

No one can afford to carry on ignoring what the Bible says. These passages were not written for the generations to come, or even our own generation only, just to frighten us here on earth. No! But as a warning, because they will come to pass without fail. Whatever God says will happen. As the Word leaves God's mouth it will accomplish all He desires, see Isaiah 55:11.

God told Moses to write down His Words, and God Himself wrote on tablets of stone the first Ten Commandments, so that they would be heeded by all the inhabitants of His Creation; see Exodus 32:16. It says: ***Now the tablets were the work of God and the writing was the writing of God engraved on the tablets***. (Wow, can you imagine? The Lord wrote His own words for the following generations to obey.)

It says in Isaiah 40:8: *The grass withers, the flower fades, but the Word of our God stands forever.* And in Matthew 5:18: *For truly I tell you* (the Lord Jesus speaking), *until heaven and earth disappear not the smallest letter, not the least stroke of pen, will by any means disappear from the Law until everything is accomplished.*

These are the two greatest commandments Jesus left us (see Mark 12:30–31). The first is: *Love the Lord Your God with all your heart, with all your mind, with all your soul and with all your strength.* The second is: *Love your neighbour as yourself.* It does not mean just the people near you, but all people—especially those who have the same faith as you do.

Sometimes when people are bombarded with life's burdens and heaviness and all sorts of problems, they don't know where to turn to. They go on drinking, smoking, eating, exercising—anything that makes their mind forget some of the troubles they've been facing—thinking their problems will go away. But they don't, they remain with them from the start of their day, and years go by without any change or satisfaction in life.

Some people don't believe God exists because they can't see God with their natural eyes. But because you can never see your spirit or soul (as you can see your body) it doesn't mean you should put no importance on it. Make sure that your soul and spirit will go to heaven where you intend to stay, when you end this journey on earth.

Life on earth is a short journey; it only remains until your physical body stops functioning, while the spirit of each man will go on living forever, for eternity. And you know what? You don't have to pay with your hard-earned money or effort on your part, when you take the Word and Hand of God He's offering you.

Jesus' heart is connected with God's Hand, and there are no strings attached. What you will be getting is the certainty of having everlasting life in heaven, and the peace of heart and mind, while you are still on earth. It's satisfying to the soul.

Sometimes people's perception and pride stop them from acknowledging there is God. You might be thinking to yourself, "My friends and relatives will think I am mad if I put my trust in God," and you may be thinking, "How could I trust the invisible? I can't see God." Let me explain this to you: all people have a soul. If you don't have a soul, you do not have a will or emotions and a mind of your own. And although you cannot see your soul, you can curb it at times. Like when you're trying to go on a diet and your taste buds are craving for something, like chocolates, and your mind contradicts your emotions and now you're thinking, "Oh those calories are not good for my diet," and you pick up a banana and eat that instead. By doing that you have managed to curb your soul. In that case you have submitted your emotions (your feelings) to the good judgement of your mind.

Your soul consists of your will, your mind, and your emotion. Your soul is very important to God as your spirit will go back to God at your death. The soul of every human being is the one the Lord is trying to revive and rescue from the hands of the devil (our enemy, and enemy of God too) from the time humans sinned. It is your soul that has the senses and feels the pain, the sadness, the shame, the jealousy, the bitterness, and the joy, the contentment, the safety, the happiness, the fulfilment, the peace, etc. From the beginning of time the devil opened up the man's and the woman's natural senses. They felt the fear in the Garden so they hid themselves from God, and they felt the shame so they put a covering on themselves; there was an immediate invisible separation from their relationship with God. Before sin entered the Garden they communicated with God without barriers, emotionally and physically. The minute they obeyed the voice of the devil an invisible barrier between God and them was felt by both sides.

That is why **your soul is the part of you that the devil is trying to capture**. When you obey the devil continually you will never know how to break free from his devices, because we are feeling beings. The enemy is using our human senses for us to elude God's grace. The enemy brings havoc on what we see, feel, touch, smell, and hear. He uses our senses to give short term happiness, like taking drugs, eating too much, and keeping your mind busy. He stimulates your emotions by enticing you to see sensual acts or pornographic scenes. Your eyes are the gateway to your emotions, enabling you to awaken your sensual desire to fantasize and stir up ungodly thoughts and feelings. When you take drugs you may feel high for a while, but you're soon back to real life again and then you feel even lower than before you took that drug. Then when you start thinking in your right mind it makes you feel disgusted with yourself.

Every time you do things that you know you shouldn't do, because you know it's wrong, but you carry on doing it in that particular situation, the enemy has taken your soul captive.

And that is his strategy to keep you working, and not resting. He always stimulates human's senses, to keep you going, and hankering after something you could never fulfil, and he has no intention of stopping you, because he wants you to be busy with everything he stirs you up to do, so that your focus is always on yourself. You may feel temporarily happy at times, but with weariness and no peace in your mind; he never wants you to relax and shift your thoughts on God.

But the Lord Jesus said, *"Come to Me all you who are heavy laden and I will give you rest* (Jesus is inviting you to come closer to Him to stop you from feeling weary in your souls) *for My yoke is easy and My burden is light* (for being with His presence is refreshing and you will find peace being with Him). He also said, *"Be still and know that I am God, I will be exalted among the nations, I will be exalted on the earth"* (Psalm 46:10). *Do not fear for I Am with you, I will strengthen you and help you, I will uphold you with My righteous right Hand* (Isaiah 41:10). *The Lord says, ask for the ancient paths ask where the good way is, and walk in it, and **you will find rest for your souls*** (see Jeremiah 6:16).

God's words declared we will be at peace and at rest if we obey and follow His instruction. But the enemy would like to keep us busy, so we don't even think that there is God who loves us, and wants us to have a close relationship with Him, as we place our hope and trust in His unfailing love.

God gave us a conscience; that is the mind of our spirit, that's our inner thoughts (the right thoughts) that if open to the Holy Spirit's leading could make the right decision for our own soul. The Holy Spirit of God will always bring you near God. That is why accepting the Lord Jesus' invitation to live in your heart is a must! And you cannot go to heaven with your **human soul**, it's **enmity with God**; you can only reach heaven through a personal relationship with Jesus Christ. The moment you believe in your heart that He rose victoriously from the dead for you, your new life begins with Him, and you make Him your Lord and Saviour. It corresponds to the truth that your life is now hidden in Christ through your faith in Him (see Colossians 3:3). Our spirit is free to collaborate with the Holy Spirit, because our spirit comes from God, who gave us freewill.

When the real exchange has taken place between you and God, you become His child and He is your ever loving Father God, who cares for you, and supplies what you need. But you still have to ask Him in prayer for what you need. He does not presume, He waits for you to tell Him what you need; and He never ever violates your freewill, that's why the relationship He's offering you is easy, not burdensome.

God doesn't crush your will. You always have a free choice, not a restricted one just to do His will, but allowing you a choice to obey if you can. And if you're not ready to obey He gives you a concession to stay in contact with Him; the Holy Spirit will nudge you to stay closer. He will never ever drive you away, or shut the door in your face, to let you walk away without nudging your heart to see sense. He always wants you to come to Him with an open and honest heart, and to enjoy His company and protection.

God doesn't want you to try and hide anything from Him. He can see your heart anyway, so it means you cannot hide it from Him. He is abounding in love and never wants you to have pain in your soul and have a barrier between you and Him, so that it won't stop you coming closer to Him. **He will always revive your soul when you feel weary in this world we are in**.

Because God loves us and treats us as His children, and those He treats as His, He chastens and rebukes. If He never reproofs you, you are not His child; you are illegitimate. (See Revelation 3:19.) The Lord Jesus wants to handle you like breakable glass, because when you're broken inside that's when He mends your wounded soul. He gave us allowance for our own good and not to drive us away from Him, even if we didn't obey Him. **He loved us first** while we were still sinners and accepts us for who we are. He intended to reflect His heart to us as a loving Father! God's perfect love for us does not consist of the good things we did or our obedience to Him.

So because you are known by Him, He is now inviting you to be with Him forever to the place we call heaven. There's a party in heaven and your name is written on the invitation card in Jesus' heavens! If you do not know and do not believe or recognise God in your life, the invitation is for you and all your loved ones. And He is the host of the party! Everybody is welcome. Come, come just as you are! He's so, so, excited to have you come, not as a guest only, not just as a participant, but as a permanent resident. What are you waiting for, Christmas? **The first Christmas will not come again**, but **His second coming is soon**; don't delay, come quickly, His arms are widely open to receive you. He's waiting for you to make that decision.

Do not let the enemy have anything to accuse you of the sin pre-loaded in your head. If you look at the Bible it will tell you in Psalm 103:12: *As far as the east is from the west, so far has He removed our transgressions from us.* So long as you ask the Lord Jesus to forgive all your sins, when the enemy is trying to accuse you of your sin in the face of our Saviour Jesus, the Lord will answer him and will say, "What sin? They repented and I have forgiven them; all their sins are erased, covered by My blood; they are justified, they're My children; and I promised them that they would be with Me forever."

No unclean thing can enter heaven, but by the blood of God's Son, you are separated and cleansed.

15

YOUR BENEFITS HERE ON EARTH AS YOU BELIEVE IN GOD'S WORD

There are times when we have to put into practice what we believe, if it is true and not just a word that we hear, and if there is any value, or benefit we can draw out of it.

I know a lot of people would say that *to see is to believe*. I'm talking of nature versus faith. Nature is what you do not have to believe—it is all there as you see it; you hear it, you touch it, you smell it, you taste it. But it says in Hebrews 11:1: ***Now faith is the substance of things hoped for, the evidence of things not seen***. Now you may ask, "What is *substance*?" The dictionary definition is: *the real physical matter of which a person or thing consists and which has a tangible, solid presence*. And I'm telling you, when God is about, you will definitely feel His presence. It's drawing you to it, it's absorbing you and it is so peaceful. You may ask, how? When the Holy Spirit of God is present, you will connect to it because of the spirit within you. As I mentioned, every living being has a spirit, and that spirit, which is from God, will connect to the Holy Presence of God.

Faith hope is a real hope; it is not the hope that consists in wishful thinking. According to the passage above it's a deeper kind of hope, a hope where you're expectant for solid evidence. A hope that anchors to something bigger and higher than you, and where else can you anchor that hope, but in God, and in the Holy Spirit who works behind the scenes as we call on Him.

Let me just explain the way I know. When I hope for something I want, like a wishy-washy wish, which is not hope at all (some people might take that as hope), for example: I want to visit Taj Mahal, or the Andes or the Himalayas or New York, or wherever else I want to go, that is achievable, assuming I have the money and time. I depend on myself, and it's within my reach. While the hope that is of faith, which is biblical hope, is something that you can only experience depending on whom, or where, you anchor or pin your expectation onto. It's outside of your own ability, that no matter what you do in the natural it would not shift or budge; no amount of your ability could help you. The hope where you have to know where you are firmly established and anchored to is the biblical hope I'm talking about here. And for me that is no other than putting my hope in God, who has the power to act beyond what I can do. I could ask of Him and He will do it because He is God of His Word and God of His Standard—not according to humans' incapability or capability, but according to God's nature.

Then I suppose you may ask, what is the nature of God? More than what I know; but what I know of Him let me tell you: He is a God of Love, He is an Almighty God, Omnipotent and all Powerful. He is an Omnipresent God, He is Omniscient, He is the Alpha and the Omega, the beginning and the end, who so loved me and died for me, and He's a healing God. When I put my hope in God, who is what I mentioned about Him in the above, I will always be on the winning side.

How can one have hope in God? You have to know Him. To know Him is to have a relationship with Him. And that's why I'm persuading you all along in the previous chapters of this book, that anyone could have a relationship with Him. One thing for sure, as the Lord Jesus said in John 6:44: *"No one can come to Me unless the Father who sent Me draws them to Me, and I will raise them up at the last day."* In this passage you will see there is a promise that the Lord Jesus himself said, *"I will raise you up in the last day."* What is this last day, you may ask? This is the day when the Lord will gather all whom Father God draws to Him and come to Him on the **judgement day**. And for those people whom Father God draws but they refuse to go near or come to the Lord Jesus, they have no hope. You might say, "How I can be near God"? Well, He is as close to you as the folding of your hands and the closing of your eyes and calling Him. Call Him from your heart and He will be there; He will never drive you away.

Let me give you a little example of the kind of deeper hope a little mouse had in himself, from the film, 'Gruffalo'. Whenever this little wood-mouse felt scared of the other animals he met that were bigger than him, like the fox, the owl, and the snake, who all invited him for lunch—really to eat him—he would keep on making up stories. He would say to each of them that he was on his way to meet 'Gruffalo'. He would describe this imaginary creature to them, whose favourite food was always the creature in front of him. He said to the fox, "Gruffalo's favourite food is roasted fox." To the owl, "Gruffalo's favourite food is owl ice cream," and to the snake, "Gruffalo's favourite food is scrambled snake." So in this way the little mouse escaped from their grasp. These three creatures he met eventually meet each other in the woods and they find out that the mouse has outwitted them, and he was only making up stories about meeting this Gruffalo—with terrible teeth and terrible claws, knobbly knees and turned-out toes, with a poisonous wart at the end of his nose, his eyes are orange, and his tongue is black and he has purple prickles all over his back!

When he meets these creatures again he doesn't show he fears them. The mouse carries on walking through the woods until he meets the real Gruffalo, who turns out to be exactly the same as the terrible creature he described to the other animals in the woods. And the Gruffalo says to the mouse, "You taste good with a slice of bread." But this brainy little mouse replies to the Gruffalo, "You know, I ... I am the scariest creature in the woods," and persuades the Gruffalo to walk with him. So Gruffalo agrees and as they are walking through the woods Gruffalo hears the hiss of the snake. When the snake sees the Gruffalo he takes one look at him following behind the mouse and then says goodbye to the mouse. When the owl sees the mouse again he's about to grab him with his claws, but the mouse says, "Well, hello owl," and holds his head high. When the owl sees the Gruffalo behind he flies off in fear of Gruffalo. As they carry on their way the fox comes along too and sees the mouse with the Gruffalo behind him. Scared of the Gruffalo, he too quickly says goodbye to the mouse. "Well, Gruffalo," the mouse said, "everyone is afraid of me," and makes his loudest growl at him. He then comes closer to Gruffalo and whispers that his favourite food is Gruffalo crumble, so Gruffalo runs off in fear. Then the little mouse peacefully returns to the acorn he found earlier and eats it.

What I am trying to show here is in your life you might face some frightening or worrying experiences, but if you know God, the Big God, the Almighty God and His power, who holds your life in the palm of His hands, and so loves you for who you are, your big problems will become smaller. If you accept Him who will have solutions for all your problems, all you need to do is to call on Him, and let Him have a say in your life; let Him guide and lead you. At times you may feel scared but if you put your trust in Him, He will never ever let you down.

The following are some examples of the benefits you have as a Christian, taken from my diary. You get faith by hearing the Word of God and experiencing it as I did in these previous years as a born-again believer. So here are the things that I can share with you, the experiences I had with other people who were not even believers yet, or on the verge of becoming believers in Christ Jesus.

Today, 19th of January 2011, I was praying for the believers in the Maldives after reading the persecuted church prayer requests. I feel the Lord wanted me to pray that these people would have an indelible connection with the Lord. I did not know what that word indelible meant until I looked it up in the dictionary, and this is the meaning: *Incapable of being erased or obliterated, or indestructible.* I heard this word indelible directly from the Lord. Thank You, Lord, how awesome You are, O my God.

Way back in 2011 when I was training at The Healing Rooms, one Thursday in February someone told me this is what he heard for me from the Lord: "The Lord loves you, Naylee, with an everlasting love. The Lord wants to speak to you in your spirit everyday through the Holy Spirit." He continued prophesying to me saying that I will hear the beat of the Lord's heart and that I am His—belonging to God. Also this lady told me "the Lord is touching my chin" and "it was growing up time for me," and "the Lord will give me the spirit of prophecy and I will speak when the Lord wants me to speak and I will be quiet when I don't hear anything from God."

I also felt in the Healing Rooms, during the time of worshipping on the 17th of March 2011, the Lord is anointing each and every one with what we are capable of carrying. The following day, Friday, before going to work, I didn't feel like washing my hair because the Lord anointed me in the Healing Rooms the previous day. But right there and then, when I was contemplating this in my head, **I heard the Holy Spirit say to me, "My anointing is not counterfeit."**

Another time at the Healing Rooms sessions, someone told me, "This is what the Lord is telling me: 'Listen, O daughter, consider and give ear, forget your people and your father's house. Honour Him for He is your Lord.'"

All sorts of things sometimes entered my mind while I was at the Healing Rooms, worshipping. Once, in my mind, I thought, "I cannot get any word from the Lord." All of a sudden I heard a noise of a hand-held fan being opened and closed sharply, then a loud clap near the right side of my ear, and **I heard the Holy Spirit speak to me and say, "Snap out of it."** Of wrong thoughts about not hearing God, because I know I do! It was God's work; I could not invent the loud clap. It made me jump a bit and the opening and closing of the fan sharply truly snapped me out of my thoughts. I wasn't fearful, so I became confident that the Lord was stopping me from focusing on what I was thinking, and then He helped me. I needed an effort to focus my mind on God and not on what I know is not of God, so that I could hear Him.

It was the 27th of March 2011, and I was at our Sunday evening service where there was a 'soaking in the Spirit' meeting. I was lying on a pew, wanting to hear what the Spirit of the Lord was saying to us, as a church. All of a sudden I heard lots and lots of fireworks going off outside the church. I really thought that some people just wanted to let some fireworks off, left-over fireworks from New Year's Eve and they just wanted to use them up. This was until I asked two people in the meeting on that night if they heard the fireworks going off for quite a while. Both of them said they hadn't heard anything. It was loud, but no one heard them apart from me, so I realised my spiritual ears were open! After all, it was March; there shouldn't be any fireworks going off then. I was thinking, of course it is not New Year—that's long gone. I knew then that the fireworks I heard were in the spirit realm.

When I got home I asked the Lord what was the meaning of these fireworks, and I heard the Lord give me the impression

'New Year for our church' and that 'the Lord is blowing cobwebs off people's lives'. On that Sunday evening I had a dream about fireworks, and it was the same meaning, 'New Year for the church', the Lord is blowing cobwebs off the lives of people **and there would also be a celebration.** This was now the morning of the 28th of March 2011. One of our church members got a word on that soaking in the spirit night: 'New beginnings for us as a church'. So what I heard confirmed this message.

And today, the 13th of April 2011, I was fasting for our church growth and the new beginning the Lord wanted to bring to us, His people. As I was having a shower the Lord reminded me of the vision I saw, way back in 2005, where the Lord Jesus was so massive on the Cross, but so tiny on the earth, perplexed because we don't do what we say we are going to do. I reflected on the point where we say our God loves us, and we love Him too, but our actions towards Him does not show to unbelievers that He is the big God we know. I suppose we became a bit blasé because we just focus on God's love for us, and that we are so important to Him as His children, that we forget that He is an Almighty God, who needs to be revered and honoured. Some conform to the pattern of this world, and when the Lord looks down from heaven and sees our behaviour, He cannot distinguish us from the unbelievers. But the Lord is bringing change to us as a church of God. For there are still those who want to obey God's purpose for us.

On the 24th of April 2011, we were soaking in the spirit again, on the last Sunday of the month as usual, and as I was lying there waiting for the Holy Spirit for what He was going to do or say, I heard lots and lots of furniture moving about; and as I heard this I saw the minister and others moving the furniture. I asked the Lord what it meant, and **I felt the Lord was saying, "Make room, make room."**

On the 5th of May 2011, as we were worshipping at the Healing Rooms before the sessions started, I smelled the essence of a medicine and I felt the Lord was saying, "I will bring healing to these people," and quite a few of them weren't well. When I asked the Lord what word He had for us today, I sensed He was telling me, "**I am the Lord who heals.**"

On Saturday the 21st of May 2011, my husband went to Los Angeles on a business trip for a week. As I was praying for myself, on my own again for the first time after 14 years together, I just felt the peace of God. Complete peace and I knew everything would be just fine. On that evening he arrived in Los Angeles, but as he never goes anywhere on his own he wasn't feeling good and he was jet lagged and extremely tired; he didn't feel good at all. So I prayed again for him and I encouraged him with what I felt the Lord was saying to him. I told him, "**God is closer to you than any human being could ever be. Because he lives in you and is in your heart**," and I also felt the Lord calling, "My son, you are precious to Me, I am carrying you, though you may not feel it. You will look back and see My Hand upon you strengthening you and upon your situation too. So be encouraged." I told him that "He is with you and doing a new thing for you." You see, there's comforting words you can hear from God when you put your trust in Him.

On Sunday the 19th of June 2011 I was invited to a birthday party which I could not come to until a lot later, as I was supposed to be working that day. But before I could even leave the church I had a terrible pain in my stomach, I still felt unable to go to work. So I phoned to cancel my overtime as I wasn't well enough to work. Two hours later I was well enough to go to the party, so I went and met a friend there whom I didn't know was also a friend to this lady who invited us both. I shouldn't have met her there as I was supposed to come late and she would have left before I arrived, if things had happened as we planned. But I believe the Lord had planned it for us to meet on that particular day.

She was a close friend to one of our mutual friends and she told me she was ill but had never said anything to her close friends yet. She asked me to pray for her as she knew I went to church every Sunday. So I promised her I would pray and I invited her to my house on the following Wednesday. I didn't realise my husband would have a day off on that day till I looked at my calendar, so I cancelled. But she had a doctor's appointment on that Wednesday anyway, but because she said yes to see me at home on that day, she was a bit apprehensive to cancel our meeting. Then I realised Thursday would be better for me, so I phoned her back and then she told me that Thursday was also the best day for her to meet me.

So on Thursday the 23rd of June 2011 she came to my home. I prayed for her and asked her if she wanted to accept the Lord Jesus as her Lord, personal Saviour, protector and healer of her life. She accepted, and also she accepted the Holy Spirit to be her guide in life from that day on.

She was the first person I led in prayer to the Lord Jesus' Salvation. I also asked her if she wanted to come to our church meetings, and she agreed. I told her she could bring her husband and he could also accept the Lord in his life as his Saviour. They both came to church on that Sunday, the 26th of June 2011. From then on they both attended our church regularly, and her husband accepted the Lord the following Sunday, the 3rd of July 2011. From then on **they said church life for them has become a lifestyle. It's a day of the week they both look forward to, and it has changed them both.** They used to go to a car rally almost every Sunday, but now they both go to meet with the Lord every Sunday or whenever they are free to come to a church meeting. They tasted the power of the Holy Spirit in their lives through our church and they said, "It's so amazing." The peace and inner joy that enveloped them, and us all, in our church is so real. It's unreal in the natural world we are living in now.

Without God and the Lord Jesus, and the power of the Holy Spirit, life is meaningless. Life is just work, work, work; no rest. As a result of their experiencing God's goodness in their lives they invited their friends along, including a gentleman whom she met at work. And today we are all members of the same church, together with two other Filipina friends of ours. Sadly one of them passed away five years ago.

Today we are all members of a church where when you walk in you feel you're a part of a family. I am not praising our church, not at all, because we are all, just like you are, imperfect people, but we are trying our best to welcome anyone who walks in as a part of the church family.

This next section, again taken from my diary, is about the experiences I had with people that are not even believers in the

Lord Jesus' healing, and not even church goers, but received healing from the Lord through my faith in God. For this is what scripture promises:

But for you who revere My name, the sun of righteousness will rise with healing in its wings (Malachi 4:2). In Matthew 4:23: *Jesus went throughout Galilee, teaching in their synagogues, proclaiming the good news of the kingdom, and healing every disease and sickness among the people.* And in Jeremiah 33:6: *Nevertheless, I will bring health and healing to it; I will heal my people and will let them enjoy abundant peace and security.*

Sometime this year, 2015, there was a lady who was in terrible pain with her back. She almost looked angry because of the pain she was experiencing. So I offered to pray for her, and she allowed me. A few weeks later she came back to me and said, "You know you prayed for me, I don't have pain anymore in my back." Later on I found out her name was Vicky. I saw her again about two years later, and I asked how her back was. She replied, "Since you prayed for me, I've never had any back pain, and I could testify that prayer works."

I work in a supermarket where I meet a lot of very ordinary people, like you and me, and I have the privilege of talking to them and sometimes praying for them too, though not always. It started when this lady, who I once saw in our church meeting, came to my till and as we were talking she said she had a terrible headache. So I just said, "Can I pray for you?" "Yes," she said; then I said, "Put your hand on your head and I will pray for you." So she did, and after I prayed we continued talking and after a while she said, "My head doesn't feel so tight now." This was before I started to join in praying for people in the Healing Rooms.

March 21st 2015, this lady and her husband came to my till and the lady talked to me so openly about the bad experience she had when she was little, and I only served her for the first time, as far as I remember. When she was about to pay she told me she had arthritis in her right thumb. She found it hard to pull out her visa card. So I asked her if I could pray for her thumb. I told her to grab her arthritic thumb with her other hand and I would pray for her. So she did and I prayed for her. After a while she said, "Oh, I can move it a bit, it doesn't hurt as bad as it did."

On the 26th of March 2015, Thursday, we were singing songs of praise at the healing room. We bowed down and confessed, "You are Lord in this place," and I felt I had to kneel down. So I did and the next minute I heard myself **praying in tongues** (speaking in a heavenly language). I didn't know what I was saying, but I know the Lord knew. He enabled me to speak that language at that time.

At work, on the 28th of March, I saw this lady I had prayed for a week earlier, and her husband. They came to my till again. I asked her about her thumb and she said, "It's not one hundred percent," so I prayed again the same thing. I said to her, "Hold your thumb with your other hand and I will pray again." On the 18th of April 2015, I saw her again and I asked how her thumb was. She said, "It's completely healed." So praise the Lord, God answers prayers. After I prayed, the Lord so graciously healed her of her arthritis. I was so excited; I remember I kept on praying that the people I will be praying for will get healed instantly.

On the 3rd of April 2015, the day before Good Friday, before I went to work, I felt the Lord was saying to me, "Deny yourself." Fast for a day, this is what I feel the Lord was telling me. I had that impression the day before too, but I was not a hundred percent sure. I was thinking, "Oh, it's Good Friday tomorrow, I will have fish." But that day, Good Friday, I felt the Lord was repeating what He asked of me the day before, to deny myself of food, so I did.

I didn't ask the Lord what it was for, but it entered my head that the Lord wanted me to fast for the salvation of this man and his mother who always talked to me when I'm serving them at the shop where I work. I was already praying for them since the man told me about his dream of heaven, and a Voice told him that if he dies he will go to the other place which, I believe, is not heaven. But he thinks it's just a place. They are not believers, although I found out they are of Jewish descent. I know salvation comes from the Jews, as the Lord Jesus, the Messiah, is a Jew. So I became happier to pray and even fast for them as the Lord instructed me. I'm grateful for the Jews, and although it's not through them personally why I believe in the Lord Jesus as the Saviour of the world, salvation started from the Jews anyway.

The following day, Saturday, this Jewish man and his mum came to my till again, and as we were talking I asked them how they were. The man said he had a pain in the back of his neck. He had had arthritis for six years and now he wasn't feeling too good, especially when driving long distances. I asked if I could pray for his neck, and he said, "Yes." So I told him, "Put your hand where your pain is and I will pray for you," so he did. After I prayed, he said, "I felt the heat on the back of my neck as you were praying; it seems to be a different kind of heat." When I asked if the pain was still there, he said, "Yes." I felt the Lord ask me to pray again, but I got a bit apprehensive to do it again because by this time I had a customer queuing to be served. I didn't have another chance to pray again. He told me sometimes the pain is bearable, but he didn't want to know after that, so I didn't pray again.

A week later I gave this gentleman a Bible called 'The Voice'. I know one may only get Jewish people's attention when they see the result immediately. Unfortunately his healing didn't take place straight away. Nevertheless, I told him, "God heals, you know, check it out," and gave him the Bible.

On the 24th of April 2015, in the early hours of the morning at home, I had a dream I was singing and the song goes:

Only Jesus is the answer, only Jesus can heal ... He has shown you great compassion, He will build you within. Only Jesus is the answer, only Jesus can hear.

That day I was worried about this mother and son whom I gave the Bible to. As I was praying in the early hours of the morning I felt the Lord was saying, "My Word." I woke up early Saturday morning and I heard, "My Word will not return to Me void but it will accomplish what I have sent it for." (See Isaiah 55:11.)

Today, June 13th 2015, Saturday, I prayed for a customer, for his backache. He said he and his wife are both Roman Catholics.

When I was praying for him, I didn't ask him if he is a believer, yet I sensed in my spirit he is a born again Christian, so I declared, "By His stripes you are healed." He said "Amen." Two weeks later I saw him again, and asked him, "How is your back?" He said "A lot better, no backache."

The 13th of July 2015: I came to realise after reading Smith Wigglesworth's daily devotion, I do not need to plead with the Holy Spirit to be with me, for it says in Deuteronomy 31:6: *The Lord your God goes with you; He will never leave you nor forsake you.* And while I am writing this part, I also believe that applies to my daughter too, and all believers in the Lord Jesus Christ of Nazareth.

Today, Friday the 31st of July 2015, a lady customer came to tell me, when I was on my till, that she had pain in her right arm. "It's so painful," she complained. So I offered to pray for her, and she said while I was praying she could feel the heat in this painful arm and said the pain had lessened a bit. I prayed for her twice in the name of Jesus. The following Friday, this lady came over to me punching the air, and said to me, "Look, look—the pain is gone." She also told me that she told her husband what had happened. She told me the pain lessened in the night, but when she woke up the following day Saturday morning the pain had completely gone. "Thank you," she said. I asked her name and she replied, "Sharon."

On Sunday, the 30th of August 2015, a word came to mind today while we were in church: 'The cleansing Power of the Blood of Jesus can cleanse us all from our guilty feeling and shame. The Lord is the way forward'. You know, God does talk to His people, for it says in Psalm 25:14: *The Lord confides in those who fear him; He makes his covenant known to them.*

On the 14th of November 2015 it came to mind, as if the Lord wanted me to know, when the adversary puts a bad thought in my mind, like past hurts, or wrong attitudes towards others etc. or even when the thought of illness comes to mind, "Tell the enemy, 'Don't you dare entice me to do your bad works for you at my own expense; depart from me, for you are a defeated foe by the Lord Jesus from the beginning of the world. Depart and go into the pit where you belong; do not crawl back out but stay in there, in the Name of Jesus, Amen.'"

The Lord gave me a fighting thought, to defeat the enemy's insistence of entertaining wrong perceptions in my mind, and not to open my gateway for the enemy's bad ideas for me. So if you are reading this part of my book and you are a believer in God, you too have a power to resist the thoughts that the devil is trying to let you entertain in your head, against you or against your own family. Fight it with God's Word. The protection of the Lord is upon His people. Away from me you devil, in Jesus' mighty name, Amen.

On Friday, the 27th of November 2015, a lady at work named Lynda had a frozen shoulder. She told me she was supposed to have an injection on the coming Tuesday for it. I felt sorry for her because she had been in pain for some time as I had heard her complain about it before. I didn't know if she knew I am a Christian but I asked her if I could pray for her and she said, "Yes." I said, "Put your hand where your pain is and I will pray for you in the name of Jesus." The following Friday Lynda said, "Thank you, Naylee, thank you; my pain is gone. I asked her if she went to hospital. "No," she said, "I don't need to—my pain is gone!" I was so excited that the Lord had released her from her frozen shoulder. Thank You, Lord. She is the third lady so far the Lord has healed this year. So praise You, Lord.

At work, on the 12th of Dec. 2015, I asked the Lord today if He wanted me to pray for this boy whose arm was in a sling. I heard the Lord say, "The world is your oyster." So I asked the boy's mum what had happened to his arm. She said he had been in plaster for over two months now and he was still in pain, and with Christmas so near she hoped he would enjoy all the things that are going on. I told his mother I knew just the One who could heal him; I clicked my finger and said, "Just like that." And I asked if I could pray for him, and she turned and asked him, and he nodded. So I told him to put his hand on his arm, but he grimaced and said it was painful; so I just prayed anyway.

The next time I saw him, when they came to my till, he had no sling on his arm. He didn't say anything, neither did his mum, but she sort of smiled at me. I didn't ask them what had happened as it was so busy at the checkout, but I knew for sure the Lord had graciously healed his arm. I didn't want them to feel intimidated by me, so I didn't ask. Praise the Lord anyway.

The Lord's healing is freely given to us, to all those who believe and to those who have been prayed for by a believer. **All we have to do is take the Lord Jesus at His Word.** His word is life, His word is Power, His word is healing. And we do not need to plead for our healing; that is Father God's main purpose for sending His Only Son on the Cross. It is for our healing and salvation and relationship with Him who rescued us from all fears and illnesses. You can receive healing from your physical, mental, emotional, and even spiritual symptoms. Spiritual—where no amount of medicine you take will affect you and you will not get healed of it.

Example: Matthew 17:14–20: *A man came to Him* (Jesus), *kneeling down to Him and saying, "Lord, have mercy on my son, for he is an epileptic and suffers severely; for he often falls into the fire and often into the water. So I brought him to Your disciples, but they could not cure him."*

Then Jesus answered and said, "O faithless and perverse generation, how long shall I be with you? How long shall I bear with you? Bring him here to Me." And Jesus rebuked the demon, and it came out of him; and the child was cured from that very hour.

Then the disciples came to Jesus privately and said, "Why could we not cast it out?"

So Jesus said to them, "Because of your unbelief; for assuredly, I say to you, if you have faith as a mustard seed, you will say to this mountain, 'Move from here to there,' and it will move; and nothing will be impossible for you. **However, this kind does not go out except by prayer and fasting."**

You may be thinking, if the disciples could not cast out the demon when they were with the Lord Jesus, what chance have we of casting out demons?

In Mark 16:17–18: ***These signs will accompany those who believe. In my name*** *they will cast out demons and will speak in* *new tongues. They will pick up snakes with their hands; and when they drink deadly poison, it will not hurt them at all;* **they will place their hands on sick people, and they will get well.**"

But we Christians are not against anyone seeking medical help, as God provided the doctors with knowledge to prescribe the right medicine. We too seek the doctor's advice when we need it.

At work today a customer looked like she was in extreme pain—body and soul. It was very cold outside but she was wearing only summer clothing. She told me she had just come out of hospital that morning, weeping as she spoke. She said, "There's no one to help me, not even to do my shopping."

When I saw her in pain I couldn't help but to extend compassion to her, so I asked if I could pray for her, and she agreed. And then in the end I gave her a blessing from a passage in the Bible: Numbers 6:24–26, and declared Shalom, an all wellbeing of body, soul, and spirit—from the Lord of course. What I recited to her originated from the priestly blessing the Lord taught Aaron, the priest of God. She then welled up. After all, she was just going shopping to get food, when this woman at the till sent a prayer to God for her and spoke Christian blessings of wellbeing over her.

Today, the 11th of February 2016, at the Healing Rooms as we were worshipping I saw this word: Bene, Bene, Bene. I asked the Lord what it meant: *Good, Good, Good.*

Two clients today, a husband and wife, were the two people that I had invited to the Healing Rooms many times before, but they had never managed to come; but today they both did. The husband, a customer of mine, came to my till and as we talked he mentioned that his wife was ill in hospital. He said that she had this bleeding for a while in the lower part of the brain that ran down to her spine, and she had been in agony for days. He was so scared and worried. So I told him we would pray for her at our home group meeting, and we did. The next time he spoke to me, he said that his wife was now at home, well, and back to work, and it was only a few days after we had prayed. So I reminded him that we prayed. That's why I believe they came to the Healing Rooms today. I was so excited because they both accepted the Lord Jesus as their Saviour, Protector, Healer and Lord of their lives. So Bene, Bene, Bene!

In the early hours of the morning of 19th of February 2016, I was still in bed when I heard, "Share the Word." As I was journaling this message, a thought came to mind: JESUS IS THE WORD (see John 1:1 & 2). The book of Genesis was the application of the Word. God said, "Let there be light" and light existed. When the Lord raised up Lazarus back to life, His Word was power over Lazarus' dead body. And the Lord Jesus' Word is Power to those who believe in Him and His Word. The sick people were healed through His Word. So many miracles happened in the day of the Lord Jesus here on earth and in the days of His disciples' teaching and healing. And Jesus Christ is the same yesterday, today, and forever. See Hebrews 13:8. And He is still healing today, so thank You, Lord.

Today the 21st of February 2016 a lady member of our church was talking to me, and I asked her how she was. She told me about her thumb that she could not move. I touched it and it felt hard. I told her about Eileen, a lady I had prayed for in the shop. I told her this customer had arthritis in her thumb and I prayed for her and the Lord healed her. "Can I pray for you?" I asked. She agreed, so I prayed for her while she held her own thumb. After I prayed, we both saw her thumb twitching for a while. After that she could move her thumb from side to side and she's now able to use it again; so thank You, Lord Jesus.

Today, the 22nd of February, I was watching the T.B.N. TV channel and I heard the story of an alcoholic man being transformed. The Lord had sent His Angel to this man in a prison cell and healed him of his addiction. After seeing this programme, I said to the Lord, "Lord, is that possible? You rescued this man without anyone praying for him, and he was not even talking to You either?" I heard the Lord answer me saying, "I SEE HIS HEART."

Probably this man believed in God, I don't know. I was not asking the Lord why He healed this man; I suppose I wanted to know *how*. He was probably praying in his heart, that's why the Lord told me He saw this man's heart.

So if anyone is burdened and no one is available to call on God, even if that person doesn't believe in healing or miracles, if their heart is exposed to God, without knowing it, they are really calling on Him, and God will answer. So we may know that all the glory belongs to God, not to those who prayed or got healed, but to God alone who heals.

On the 15th of March 2016, Tuesday, this customer of mine, named Jill, said she had a pain in her back. I have spoken to her many times before and she always looks happy, but this time she told me about the pain in her back. I also managed to tell her some people that the Lord had graciously healed after I prayed for them. She told me she sometimes cried at night because of the pain, so, as usual, I asked her if I could pray for her. After praying for her, I asked her if she felt any change in the pain; she said, "Not yet, we will see."

On the 18th of March, Friday, I saw her and asked if there was any change in her pain. She shook her head and said, "It didn't work." I said to myself, "I'll leave it to You Lord." On the 29th of March 2016, I was going to the canteen for my lunch break when Jill turned around and said, "I'm cured, I'm cured!" (She must have seen me before I saw her.) "What do you mean?" I said. "Thank you, thank you for praying." Then I said, "Oh, oh, I remember." So I asked her, "Did you do anything different?" "No," she replied, and thanked me again. I pointed up and said to her, "You've got someone to thank. I mean the Lord."

This was the fourth lady that came back to me saying they had got better or been healed after I prayed for them. So praise the Lord! **When I pray for myself I get healed too; so this is one of the benefits of being a believer in Christ Jesus**. Their Healer is my Healer.

Today, at Seaton, in Devon, on the 14th of July 2016, a thought come to mind that I don't need to plead for anyone's healing to take place, including myself; **it's God's will for everyone to be healed**. That's why He died on the Cross for me and you. It says in Isaiah 53:5: *But He was pierced for our* *transgressions, He was crushed for our iniquities; the punishment that brought us peace was upon Him, and **by His wounds we are healed**.* We only need to believe.

And today, the 12th of June 2018, Jill came to my till. I asked her how she was and enquired about her back. She said, "Since you prayed I don't have any pain anymore. "And how long ago is that, do you think?" I asked, "Oh," she said, "Maybe over two years," referring to her thoughts of how many years this person she knew had retired from work.

Today, the 13th of April 2016, Wednesday, I had a short dream where I saw two golden olive trees which were pouring out golden oil. And to cut a long story short, the meaning of my dream is: the trees are the Lord Jesus (being the Lord in man and the Lord of Hosts) and the Holy Spirit, who is pouring out golden oil, are two in One. The Lord Jesus, and the Holy Spirit who gives power to all believers, inspire us to do the work the Lord purposes for us to accomplish.

When we pray we need to wait on the Holy Spirit. So many Christians may be scared, or have not been taught, to seek the Holy Spirit for themselves, or may be thinking, "The Holy Spirit is so Holy, that if I make any mistake I will be killed by His Power." But that's not true at all; otherwise no one would be able to walk in the leading of the Holy Spirit in us. Remember that if Jesus didn't go to His ascension, the Holy Spirit could not come to guide and lead us. **Without the Holy Spirit our prayers don't have power at all**. We are nothing but flesh and bones and our prayers don't have power to reach heaven; it's like we're just talking to the air. But **when the Holy Spirit is at home in our hearts**, then God the Father and God the Son are with us, and answer our prayers.

Today at Horton Cross, Somerset, the 14th of April 2016, inside Burger King, I overheard two women talking. One of the women was with her husband, and she had just come out of hospital. She was telling this worker in Burger King that the doctor put metal in her throat to hold the bone. I couldn't help but to approach her and asked if I could pray, sort of looking at her husband asking for his permission. He said no, he didn't want me to, but his wife said, "Yes, please pray for me." I asked if I could put my hand on the back of her neck, which I did so gently, and I prayed for her. Her name is Rachel.

David, my husband, said, "You're very brave." I said to him if the Lord Jesus could heal anyone and I know they need healing, then all I have to do is ask for their permission and I know that God could heal them in the Name of Jesus. The fact is, I know the truth, and I have experienced the truth and healing of God. I know that God is just a call away and He responds in the Name of Jesus, which is the Only Name that is above every other Name. Jesus is the Name that can heal, and is a shield and a refuge for those who call and believe in His Name.

You may know the fact, but if you do not exercise what you know about the Lord Jesus then it's useless to you and to other people you encounter. It's like you have a sword in your scabbard, you see your enemy coming and you just say to yourself, "I've got a sword," and maybe shout at your enemy, "I've got a sword, I've got a sword;" but if you didn't even take it out from the scabbard and swing it about before your enemy then how does that help you? I don't know where I get my confidence in approaching people to pray for them.

Today the 18th of April 2017, Tuesday, at work, I was serving a customer when a couple came to my till. I saw the man holding his back twisting his face in agony. I asked his wife if he had backache. "Yes," she said. I then asked the Holy Spirit what I could do. I heard the Lord say, "Offer him a prayer." In my head I was thinking what word I could start with to say to this man. All of a sudden I heard myself saying to the man, "I can see that you are in pain, can I pray for you? Put your hand where your pain is." But he replied, twisting his face in agony, "I'm alright really," **but the wife shouted, "Put your hand on your back!"** So he did, and I prayed a simple prayer calling Father God, Lord Jesus, and Precious God the Holy Spirit to heal him. After the prayer I could see he was still in pain so I carried on praying in tongues for him.

After a while I saw him picking their shopping, helping his wife put it in their shopping bag. I leaned forward and whispered to the wife, "Ask him what he feels now." She did and he said, "Yeah, I'm alright, yeah I'm alright," half shading his face, embarrassed because he had said he was alright really in the first place before I prayed for him. And the wife lean forward to me and said to me, "I see the changes."

The wife paid for their shopping and the man pushed the trolley, walking upright with a straight back without any pain, and no twisting going on, on his face. So Praise You, Lord God of heaven and earth, who heals people and meets them in their needs. Praise You, O Lord God Almighty. How blessed I am to know You.

Today, Friday, the 28th of April 2017, at work, as I was scanning along, this woman who was waiting in the queue for me to serve her, held on to her head. As I saw her do that, I got a terrible pain in my head. I said to the Lord, "Lord, what is this?" And I heard the Lord say, "She has a headache." When it was her turn for me to scan her shopping, I heard the Holy Spirt speak to me from my inner self, "Ask her if she's got a headache." I was sort of apprehensive to ask, but it was so real that I felt if I didn't heed this voice of the Holy Spirit I would regret it so badly that I would be so remorseful and it would make me feel so bad.

So after observing her for a while, I leaned forward and asked her, "Have you got a headache?" Putting her hand on her head she said, "Terrible." "Can I pray for you?" I asked. She said, "Ah ... I'm touched." So I asked her to put her hand on her head and I prayed. She was with a friend and her friend gave me a look as if I were some sort of loony! "Shush..." she said to her friend, "she's praying for me." She looked red with fever, and while I was praying I could sense relief on her face, and she said, "Thank you, Thank you." So I put the Praise to God where it belongs and told her, "You know it's not me that healed you." I pointed my finger up and said to her, "You've got someone to thank," and I added, "Thank You Lord." She looked at me, put her hands together, looked up and said to me, "Thank You Lord." She agreed with me.

I also heard the Lord tell me to ask for her name, but I did not manage to ask her, as she was busy doing a transaction on her phone to pay for her shopping. I'm hoping that I will see her again and will be able to talk to her sometime. Thank You, Lord, for helping me to pray for her and that I don't need to regret what I didn't do!

Today, the 2nd of July 2017, Sunday, at church, a lady in my Filipino group of acquaintances came to our church with the help of another friend who invited her to be prayed for and get healing from the Lord. She has Lupus.

Lori asked me to pray for her and I sort of said to myself, "I cannot heal her," as if fear came to me that it's my responsibility to heal. Anyway, I don't recall anyone *I* have healed yet. I didn't have confidence on that day and I was trying to hide behind someone else's faith, so I asked the Holy Spirit whom I could get to pray with—or really hide behind their faith. But **I heard the Holy Spirit say to me**, "**Do not limit God**," and I felt then that if God could use a donkey, he could use me. So along with me, my friends Lori and Flor prayed for her. This lady agreed to accept the Lord as her Saviour and protector of her life, and today we are waiting to hear from her, what the Lord has done, but no news so far. (So many people accept the Lord as their Saviour and then carry on living as if they never accepted God, but God is still gracious to them I know.)

You may think you only have to pray once and get a result. What was the result? Well, she didn't come back to tell me, so I don't really know yet. But sometimes when people get better they forget who made them well, or don't remember to mention anything to anyone.

This time I think it was near the end of November, or maybe the beginning of December 2017. I was working, when I saw this man grimacing, holding onto the end of my conveyor belt at the till. I leaned forward to speak to his wife and asked her if he had a backache. He heard me ask his wife and responded, "No! I've got Crohn's disease." "Oh," I said, and in my heart I asked the Holy Spirit, "Lord, what do you want me to do?" I sensed the Lord say, "Offer him a prayer." So I said after a while, "Can I pray for you?" The man turned to his wife and said, "She is going to bless me." So I told him to put his hand on his stomach and I would pray. But he said, "Put your hand on me, you're blessing me." So I did. I then asked him his name. "Peter," he replied. "St. Peter, I'm from Wales." "Oh, ok," I said, and carried on praying for him. "Lord, You said we are to put our hands on the sick and they will recover; so I do this in obedience to Your Word, and by Your stripes, Lord Jesus, Peter is healed, in Jesus' Name, Amen."

About three weeks later, just before Christmas, a man came over to my till while his wife was putting their shopping in a bag. He said to me, "Hello." I said hello back to him. "You don't remember me, do you?" "No," I replied. "You prayed for me about three weeks ago and it's gone, it's gone. St Peter, remember?" he informed me. "Oh ... I remember ... you're the Irish man." His wife said, "Welsh." "Oh yeah, yeah," and I got so excited I just said, "Praise the Lord, thank You Lord!"

So the Lord meets people's needs whether they are practising believers or not. God is good to all.

And today, the 2nd of April 2018, I prayed for this colleague who had swollen legs and could hardly walk and is always in pain. I must admit I have prayed for her several times, and she didn't get well as I expected (so by this you know that healing is not in my ability to do), but I prayed for her, then carried on praying in tongues while we were both working. She knows about God's healing, that's why she has allowed me to pray for her over and over again; she's a Christian. A few hours after I prayed, and we were both on our lunch break, she said to me, "Thanks, Naylee, I feel a lot better," although when she was walking she still used crutches. But before I prayed I didn't see her using the crutches. However, the following day I saw her again; she was smiling at me and was walking fine—no crutches and she said she was okay and well.

And today, the 3rd of April 2018, I showed my work colleague a book I've written and she asked, "What is it all about?" And then she read the title, 'Can You Really Hear From God Nowadays'. Then she said, "I saw a program on the television and <u>there were three,</u> four including Jesus, who can do exactly what the Lord Jesus can do, healing and miracles and all that, and it has really shaken my faith." I said that it probably wasn't real healing. She insisted it was real, and they could heal too.

I went home thinking about this and it gave me an opportunity to ponder on God's word. A thought came to me of the verses in scripture about those people who claim they can heal. It says in Matthew 24:11: *Then many false prophets will rise up and deceive many.* And in verse 24: *For false Christs and false prophets will rise and show great signs and wonders, to deceive, if possible, even the elect.* And here in Revelation 16:13–14: *And I saw <u>three unclean spirits</u> like frogs coming out of the mouth of the dragon, out of the mouth of the beast, and out of the mouth of the false prophets. For they are spirits of demons, performing signs which go out to the kings of the earth and of the whole world, to gather them to the battle of the great day of God Almighty.*

So you see, the spirits of the dead kings, and false prophets who died long ago, are now trying to deceive even the elect of God. So we need to know who we are dealing with, and what the truth is. Only in the Word of the Lord Jesus Christ of Nazareth is the truth, and only that can save us. Jesus claimed, *"I AM THE WAY, THE TRUTH AND THE LIFE. NO ONE COMES TO THE FATHER* (HIS FATHER—OUR GOD) *EXCEPT THROUGH ME"* (John 14:6). And it definitely says there are three unclean spirits who are trying to deceive people. And if your faith is not strong or you do not have the Holy Spirit in you, you might get deceived by them. So watch out for all the signs that will come to the world—and they are already in the world, for this is their abode.

As Christians, we are only passing through here. Our own destiny is in God's Hand. We are pilgrims and not true residents of earth. Our true home is heaven, where righteousness and truth reside and where God is on the throne watching over us here on earth. All these things that are happening now were predicted in the Bible before they actually happened, so we, the believers in Christ, should know that only the truth of the Lord Jesus' Word will stand to the end.

Anyway, on the 29th of June this year, 2018, she insisted on wanting to read my book. So I lent it to her and when she gave it back, she gave me a positive comment and said that my faith is deeper than hers and it's given her something to think about. Moving forward with my story about this lady, last week on the 25th of October 2018, she asked where I was going after shopping, I told her, "Oh, to the Healing Rooms. What I mean is," I explained, "we pray for people, we don't heal them." "Can you pray for me?" she asked, right there and then. I responded and told her to put her hand where her pain is, which was on her hips and knee. After prayer I asked her, "Do you feel anything?" I expected her to say, "Not yet," but she actually said, "No pain, thank you." I was so excited I just said to her, "You've got someone to thank," pointing upward, and she replied, "I always do." I wanted to tell her, "Now you know why I have that deeper faith and hope in God," but I saw that she already had a customer queuing. So I left feeling blessed knowing that our God is so, so good to all people.

But there is another example I could tell you: Sometime this year in October 2018, one of my colleagues asked me to pray for her as she had been suffering from bleeding for three months. She had been to the doctor and was told her fibroids had burst, that's why she was bleeding. So when I got home I prayed for her.

A few weeks later I asked her how she was, and she told me she's getting a bit better, but she was still bleeding. At home, one afternoon my husband and I were watching the 700 Club on the T.B.N. TV channel. During the show they normally give words of knowledge from the Lord to the viewers. I heard Terry Meeuwsen, one of the presenters, say: "There's someone haemorrhaging and the Lord is healing you right now." When I heard that, immediately something within me arose and I claimed that word of healing for my friend at work.

A few days later I happened to be sitting back to back with her at work, and I managed to pray for her. It was the 26th of October (Friday) 2018, before any customers come to her till. I claimed that: "By the Lord Jesus' wounds you are healed in the name of Jesus. Your body is the Temple of the Holy Spirit; the enemy doesn't have any right to use or touch your body for his bad purposes. How very dare the enemy touch you—you are a daughter of the Living God, you belong to Him. And I continued praying for her in tongues, while she was serving the customer.

The following Tuesday, 30th of October 2018, as I was serving a customer she came over and whispered to me: "Naylee, my bleeding has completely stopped." We were both so excited and thanked God for her healing.

On that evening I recalled the word of knowledge I heard on the T.B.N. channel that I claimed for her healing. And today the 6th of November 2018 I managed to tell my colleague the time I heard the word of knowledge from the Lord, spoken through Terry Meeuwsen when she was praying about someone who was haemorrhaging, and I claimed that healing for her. Even when I was telling her, I felt the witnessing of the Holy Spirit within me.

And that's the other benefit we get as Christians, when we believe and apply what our faith dictates to our situations in life. Even when a person is not present at the certain place when God drops the thought in your spirit, you can release the power of God's healing for anyone; distance and time are not a barrier to God's healing, when we believe.

You might say, "Well, the healing you're telling me about is for other people and not for me." But I have received healing for myself, when I prayed for myself. In fact, my first practice of praying for healing was asking God for my own healing before I prayed for anyone.

Some people I know said to me, "You prayed for people and they got healed, but where are they now? They have not accepted Jesus as their Saviour, have they?" I just feel they are trying to say that God's healing is useless, because those people the Lord healed didn't accept Him as their Saviour through my prayers. Well surely not! Just because I didn't manage to lead them to accept Christ as their Saviour, then and there, that doesn't mean God's healing for those people who were in pain and had sickness in their bodies is meaningless or irrelevant. It is possible later in their lives that maybe someone along the way in life would be able to lead them to Christ.

I responded to him who asked me about this and said, "**I cannot save them.**" I did what I needed to do and that's all I can do for them, while I was working anyway.

Someone needed to perhaps talk to them, or rather pray for them properly, rather than say, "Well, they are not saved are they?" How do they know what the future holds for those the Lord has touched?

Concerning healing and miracles, in 1 Corinthians 3:5–9 the Apostle Paul said, *"What, after all, is Apollos, and what is Paul? Only servants, through whom you came to believe—as the Lord has assigned to each his task. I planted the seed, Apollos watered it,* **but God has been making it grow***. So neither the one* **who plants nor the one who waters is anything, but only God, who makes things grow***. The one who plants and the one who waters have one purpose, and they will each be rewarded according to their own labour. For we are co-workers in God's service; you are God's field, God's building."*

Another benefit of knowing God is His word is totally dependable. His word is His seal, and whatever He says written in His Word, the Bible, has power over our circumstances, to lift us up and heal us. I can also identify God as the One who loves you and keeps on loving you. We call it in my country '**Sinusuyo**.' It is a Tagalog word meaning *pursuing with great love and tenderness with empathy, to soothe away your pain*. God identifies with your pain with deep empathy and feels the pain you are feeling, and you can have immense expectation that He will hear your heart even without the exchange of words.

A relationship with God satisfies the mind, and the experience softens the heart, and is peaceful and joyful to the soul. Only God could show that kind of love towards all people on earth. He doesn't choose people with better colour skin, or better colour eyes or the good looking ones only. God's love could touch even a heart of stone, and it would get melted away in His loving Arms ….

What I am saying is, **the benefit you get when you become a born-again believer outweighs everything you have ever known and experienced**.

A lot of people would say, "I know God." Knowing that there is God is good, but personally knowing Him is the best decision you can do today. And if you want a personal relationship with the Lord Jesus, just welcome Him into your heart. In the privacy of your bedroom or in the comfort of your lounge please do this if you wish to: Place your hand on your heart and say these words (if you agree with me):

Lord Jesus, please forgive me for all the sins I have ever done; cleanse me, please, from all of them. I accept You, O Lord Jesus, as my Lord and Saviour and protector of my life. Please come into my heart and let Your Holy Spirit rule in my heart and life; thank You Lord. In Jesus' name I pray, Amen.

Stay in that place for a while, wait for the Holy Spirit to fill you with His peace and comforting presence.

If you mean what you prayed for, you will have such a peaceful sleep you never knew existed. Now you have invited the Lord Jesus into your heart, it means you have accepted His invitation, to receive eternal life.

And now I pray a blessing over you, here it is:

**"May the Lord bless you and keep you;
May the Lord make His face shine upon you,
And be gracious to you;
May the Lord turn His face towards you,
And bring you peace. In Jesus' name Amen"**

And now I, Naylee, welcome you into the family of God! Welcome, welcome, welcome; God bless you.

www.ingramcontent.com/pod-product-compliance
Lightning Source LLC
Chambersburg PA
CBHW061959070426
42450CB00025BA/1039